The United Em

W. Stewart

CONTENTS

I. INTRODUCTORY II. LOYALISM IN THE THIRTEEN COLONIES III. PERSECUTION OF THE LOYALISTS IV. THE LOYALISTS UNDER ARMS V. PEACE WITHOUT HONOUR VI. THE EXODUS TO NOVA SCOTIA VII. THE BIRTH OF NEW BRUNSWICK VIII. IN PRINCE EDWARD ISLAND IX. THE LOYALISTS IN QUEBEC X. THE WESTERN SETTLEMENTS XI. COMPENSATION AND HONOUR XII. THE AMERICAN MIGRATION XIII. THE LOYALIST IN HIS NEW HOME BIBLIOGRAPHICAL NOTE

CHAPTER I

INTRODUCTORY

The United Empire Loyalists have suffered a strange fate at the hands of historians. It is not too much to say that for nearly a century their history was written by their enemies. English writers, for obvious reasons, took little pleasure in dwelling on the American Revolution, and most of the early accounts were therefore American in their origin. Any one who takes the trouble to read these early accounts will be struck by the amazing manner in which the Loyalists are treated. They are either ignored entirely or else they are painted in the blackest colours.

So vile a crew the world ne'er saw before, And grant, ye pitying heavens, it may no more! If ghosts from hell infest our poisoned air, Those ghosts have entered these base bodies here.

So sang a ballad-monger of the Revolution; and the opinion which he voiced persisted after him. According to some American historians of the first half of the nineteenth century, the Loyalists were a comparatively insignificant class of vicious criminals, and the people of the American colonies were all but unanimous in their armed opposition to the British government.

Within recent years, however, there has been a change. American historians of a new school have revised the history of the Revolution, and a tardy reparation has been made to the memory of the Tories of that day. Tyler, Van Tyne, Flick, and other writers have all made the amende honorable on behalf of their countrymen. Indeed, some of these writers, in their anxiety to stand straight, have leaned backwards; and by no one perhaps will the ultra-Tory view of the Revolution be found so clearly expressed as by them. At the same time the history of the Revolution has been rewritten by some English historians; and we have a writer like Lecky declaring that the American Revolution 'was the work of an energetic minority, who succeeded in committing an undecided and fluctuating majority to courses for which they had little love, and leading them step by step to a position from which it was impossible to recede.'

Thus, in the United States and in England, the pendulum has swung from one extreme to the other. In Canada it has remained stationary. There, in the country where they settled, the United Empire Loyalists are still regarded with an uncritical veneration which has in it something of the spirit of primitive ancestor-worship. The interest which Canadians have taken in the Loyalists has been either patriotic or genealogical; and few attempts have been made to tell their story in the cold light of impartial history, or to estimate the results which have flowed from their migration. Yet such an attempt is worth while making--an attempt to do the United Empire Loyalists the honour of painting them as they were, and of describing the profound and far-reaching influences which they exerted on the history of both Canada and the United States.

In the history of the United States the exodus of the Loyalists is an event comparable only to the expulsion of the Huguenots from France after the revocation of the Edict of Nantes. The Loyalists, whatever their social status (and they were not all aristocrats), represented the conservative and moderate element in the revolting states; and their removal, whether by banishment or disfranchisement, meant the elimination of a very wholesome element in the body politic. To this were due in part no doubt many of the early errors of the republic in finance, diplomacy, and politics. At the same time it was a circumstance which must have hastened by many years the triumph of democracy. In the tenure of land, for example, the emigration produced a revolution. The confiscated estates of the great Tory landowners were in most cases cut up into small lots and sold to the common people; and thus the process of levelling and making more democratic the whole social structure was accelerated.

On the Canadian body politic the impress of the Loyalist migration is so deep that it would be difficult to overestimate it. It is no exaggeration to say that the United Empire Loyalists changed the course of the current of Canadian history. Before 1783 the clearest observers saw no future before Canada but that of a French colony under the British crown. 'Barring a catastrophe shocking to think of,' wrote Sir Guy Carleton in 1767, 'this country must, to the end of time, be peopled by the Canadian race, who have already taken such firm root, and got to so great a height, that any new stock transplanted will be totally hid, except in the towns of Quebec and Montreal.' Just how discerning this prophecy was may be judged from the fact that even to-day it holds true with regard to the districts that were settled at the time it was written. What rendered it void was the unexpected influx of the refugees of the Revolution. The effect of this immigration was to create two new English-speaking provinces, New Brunswick and Upper Canada, and to strengthen the English element in two other provinces, Lower Canada and Nova Scotia, so that ultimately the French population in Canada was outnumbered by the English population surrounding it. Nor should the character of this English immigration escape notice. It was not only English; but it was also filled with a passionate loyalty to the British crown. This fact serves to explain a great deal in later Canadian history. Before 1783 the continuance of Canada in the British Empire was by no means assured: after 1783 the Imperial tie was well-knit.

Nor can there be any doubt that the coming of the Loyalists hastened the advent of free institutions. It was the settlement of Upper Canada that rendered the Quebec Act of 1774 obsolete, and made necessary the Constitutional Act of 1791, which granted to the Canadas representative assemblies. The Loyalists were Tories and Imperialists; but, in the colonies from which they came, they had been accustomed to a very advanced type of democratic government, and it was not to be expected that they would quietly reconcile themselves in their new home to the arbitrary system of the Quebec Act. The French Canadians, on the other hand, had not been accustomed to representative institutions, and did not desire them. But when Upper Canada was granted an assembly, it was impossible not to grant an assembly to Lower Canada too; and so Canada was started on that road of constitutional development which has brought her to her present position as a self-governing unit in the British Empire.

CHAPTER II

LOYALISM IN THE THIRTEEN COLONIES

It was a remark of John Fiske that the American Revolution was merely a phase of English party politics in the eighteenth century. In this view there is undoubtedly an element of truth. The Revolution was a struggle within the British Empire, in which were aligned on one side the American Whigs supported by the English Whigs, and on the other side the English Tories supported by the American Tories. The leaders of the Whig party in England, Charles James Fox, Edmund Burke, Colonel Barre, the great Chatham himself, all championed the cause of the American revolutionists in the English parliament. There were many cases of Whig officers in the English army who refused to serve against the rebels in America. General Richard Montgomery, who led the revolutionists in their attack on Quebec in 1775-76, furnishes the case of an English officer who, having resigned his commission, came to America and, on the outbreak of the rebellion, took service in the rebel forces. On the other hand there were thousands of American Tories who took service under the king's banner; and some of the severest defeats which the rebel forces suffered were encountered at their hands.

It would be a mistake, however, to identify too closely the parties in England with the parties in America. The old Tory party in England was very different from the so-called Tory party in America. The term Tory in America was, as a matter of fact, an epithet of derision applied by the revolutionists to all who opposed them. The opponents of the revolutionists called themselves not Tories, but Loyalists or 'friends of government.'

There were, it is true, among the Loyalists not a few who held language that smacked of Toryism. Among the Loyalist pamphleteers there were those who preached the doctrine of passive obedience and non-resistance. Thus the Rev. Jonathan Boucher, a clergyman of Virginia, wrote:

Having then, my brethren, thus long been tossed to and fro in a wearisome circle of uncertain traditions, or in speculations and projects still more uncertain, concerning government, what better can you do than, following the apostle's advice, 'to submit yourselves to every ordinance of man, for the Lord's sake; whether it be to the king as supreme, or unto governors, as unto them that are sent by him for the punishment of evil-doers, and for the praise of them that do well? For, so is the will of God, that with well-doing ye may put to silence the ignorance of foolish men; as free, and not using your liberty for a cloak of maliciousness, but as servants of God. Honour all men: love the brotherhood: fear God: honour the king.'

Jonathan Boucher subscribed to the doctrine of the divine right of kings:

Copying after the fair model of heaven itself, wherein there was government even among the angels, the families of the earth were subjected to rulers, at first set over them by God. 'For there is no power, but of God: the powers that be are ordained of God.' The first father was the first king... Hence it is, that our church, in perfect conformity with the doctrine here inculcated, in her explication of the fifth commandment, from the obedience due to parents, wisely derives the congenial duty of 'honouring the king, and all that are put in authority under him.'

Dr Myles Cooper, the president of King's College, took up similar ground. God, he said, established the laws of government, ordained the British power, and commanded all to obey authority. 'The laws of heaven and earth' forbade rebellion. To threaten open disrespect of government was 'an unpardonable crime.' 'The principles of submission and obedience to lawful authority' were religious duties.

But even Jonathan Boucher and Myles Cooper did not apply these doctrines without reserve. They both upheld the sacred right of petition and remonstrance. 'It is your duty,' wrote Boucher, 'to instruct your members to take all the constitutional means in their power to obtain redress.' Both he and Cooper deplored the policy of the British ministry. Cooper declared the Stamp Act to be contrary to American rights; he approved of the opposition to the duties on the enumerated articles; and he was inclined to think the duty on tea 'dangerous to constitutional liberty.'

It may be confidently asserted that the great majority of the American Loyalists, in fact, did not approve of the course pursued by the British government between 1765 and 1774. They did not deny its legality; but they doubted as a rule either its wisdom or its justice. Thomas Hutchinson, the governor of Massachusetts, one of the most famous and most hated of the Loyalists, went to England, if we are to believe his private letters, with the secret ambition of obtaining the repeal of the act which closed Boston harbour. Joseph Galloway, another of the Loyalist leaders, and the author of the last serious attempt at conciliation, actually sat in the first Continental Congress, which was called with the object of obtaining the redress of what Galloway himself described as 'the grievances justly complained of.' Still more instructive is the case of Daniel Dulany of Maryland. Dulany, one of the most distinguished lawyers of his time, was after the Declaration of Independence denounced as a Tory; his property was confiscated, and the safety of his person imperilled. Yet at the beginning of the Revolution he had been found in the ranks of the Whig pamphleteers; and no more damaging attack was ever made on the policy of the British government than that contained in his Considerations on the Propriety of Imposing Taxes in the British Colonies. When the elder Pitt attacked the Stamp Act in the House of Commons in January 1766, he borrowed most of his argument from this pamphlet, which had appeared three months before.

This difficulty which many of the Loyalists felt with regard to the justice of the position taken up by the British government greatly weakened the hands of the Loyalist party in the early stages of the Revolution. It was only as the Revolution gained momentum that the party grew in vigour and numbers. A variety of factors contributed to this result. In the first place there were the excesses of the revolutionary mob. When the mob took to sacking private houses, driving clergymen out of their pulpits, and tarring and feathering respectable citizens, there were doubtless many law-abiding people who became Tories in spite of themselves. Later on, the methods of the inquisitorial communities possibly made Tories out of some who were the victims of their attentions. The outbreak of armed rebellion must have shocked many into a reactionary attitude. It was of these that a Whig satirist wrote, quoting:

This word, Rebellion, hath frozen them up, Like fish in a pond.

But the event which brought the greatest reinforcement to the Loyalist ranks was the Declaration of Independence. Six months before the Declaration of Independence was passed by the Continental Congress, the Whig leaders had been almost unanimous in repudiating any intention of severing the connection between the mother country and the colonies. Benjamin Franklin told Lord Chatham that he had never heard in America one word in favour of independence 'from any person, drunk or sober.' Jonathan Boucher says that Washington told him in the summer of 1775 'that if ever I heard of his joining in any such measures, I had his leave to set him down for everything wicked.' As late as Christmas Day 1775 the revolutionary congress of New Hampshire officially proclaimed their disavowal of any purpose 'aiming at independence.' Instances such as these could be reproduced indefinitely. When, therefore, the Whig leaders in the summer of 1776 made their right-about-face with regard to independence, it is not surprising that some of their followers fell away from them. Among these were many who were heartily opposed to the measures of the British government, and who had even approved of the policy of armed rebellion. but who could not forget that they were born British subjects. They drank to the toast, 'My country, may she always be right; but right or wrong, my country.'

Other motives influenced the growth of the Loyalist party. There were those who opposed the Revolution because they were dependent on government for their livelihood, royal office-holders and Anglican clergymen for instance. There were those who were Loyalists because they thought they had picked the winning side, such as the man who candidly wrote from New Brunswick in 1788, 'I have made one great mistake in politics, for which reason I never intend to make so great a blunder again.' Many espoused the cause because they were natives of the British Isles, and had not become thoroughly saturated with American ideas: of the claimants for compensation before the Royal Commissioners after the war almost two-thirds were persons who had been born in England, Scotland, or Ireland. In some of the colonies the struggle between Whig and Tory followed older party lines: this was especially true in New York, where the Livingston or Presbyterian party became Whig and the De Lancey or Episcopalian party Tory. Curiously enough the cleavage in many places followed religious lines. The members of the Church of England were in the main Loyalists; the Presbyterians were in the main revolutionists. The revolutionist cause was often strongest in those colonies, such as Connecticut, where the Church of England was weakest. But the division was far from being a strict one. There were even members of the Church of England in the Boston Tea Party; and there were Presbyterians among the exiles who went to Canada and Nova Scotia. The Revolution was not in any sense a religious war; but religious differences contributed to embitter the conflict, and doubtless made Whigs or Tories of people who had no other interest at stake.

It is commonly supposed that the Loyalists drew their strength from the upper classes in the colonies, while the revolutionists drew theirs from the proletariat. There is just enough truth in this to make it misleading. It is true that among the official classes and the large landowners, among the clergymen, lawyers, and physicians, the majority were Loyalists; and it is true that the mob was everywhere revolutionist. But it cannot be said that the Revolution was in any sense a war of social classes. In it father was arrayed against son and brother against brother. Benjamin Franklin was a Whig; his son, Sir William Franklin, was a Tory. In the valley of the Susquehanna the Tory Colonel John Butler, of Butler's Rangers, found himself confronted by his Whig cousins, Colonel William Butler and Colonel Zeb Butler. George Washington, Thomas Jefferson, John Adams, were not inferior in social status to Sir William Johnson, Thomas Hutchinson, and Joseph Galloway. And, on the other hand, there were no humbler peasants in the revolutionary ranks than some of the Loyalist farmers who migrated to Upper Canada in 1783. All that can be said is that the Loyalists were most numerous among those classes which had most to lose by the change, and least numerous among those classes which had least to lose.

Much labour has been spent on the problem of the numbers of the Loyalists. No means of numbering political opinions was resorted to at the time of the Revolution, so that satisfactory statistics are not available. There was, moreover, throughout the contest a good deal of going and coming between the Whig and Tory camps, which makes an estimate still more difficult. 'I have been struck,' wrote Lorenzo Sabine, 'in the course of my investigations, with the absence of fixed principles, not only among people in the common walks of life, but in many of the prominent personages of the day.' Alexander Hamilton, for instance, deserted from the Tories to the Whigs; Benedict Arnold deserted from the Whigs to the Tories.

The Loyalists themselves always maintained that they constituted an actual majority in the Thirteen Colonies. In 1779 they professed to have more troops in the field than the Continental Congress. These statements were no doubt exaggerations. The fact is that the strength of the Loyalists was very unevenly distributed. In the colony of New York they may well have been in the majority. They were strong also in Pennsylvania, so strong that an officer of the revolutionary army described that colony as 'the enemies' country.' 'New York and Pennsylvania,' wrote John Adams years afterwards, 'were so nearly divided--if their propensity was not against us--that if New England on one side and Virginia on the other had not kept them in awe, they would have joined the British.' In Georgia the Loyalists were in so large a majority that in 1781 that colony would probably have detached itself from the revolutionary movement had it not been for the surrender of Cornwallis at Yorktown. On the other hand, in the New England colonies the Loyalists were a small minority, strongest perhaps in Connecticut, and yet even there predominant only in one or two towns.

There were in the Thirteen Colonies at the time of the Revolution in the neighbourhood of three million people. Of these it is probable that at least one million were Loyalists. This estimate is supported by the opinion of John Adams, who was well qualified to form a judgment, and whose Whig sympathies were not likely to incline him to exaggerate. He gave it as his opinion more than once that about one-third of the people of the Thirteen Colonies had been opposed to the measures of the Revolution in all its stages. This estimate he once mentioned in a letter to Thomas McKean, chief justice of Pennsylvania, who had signed the Declaration of Independence, and had been a member of every Continental Congress from that of 1765 to the close of the Revolution; and McKean replied, 'You say that ... about a third of the people of the colonies were against the Revolution. It required much reflection before I could fix my opinion on this subject; but on mature deliberation I conclude you are right, and that more than a third of influential characters were against it.'

CHAPTER III

PERSECUTION OF THE LOYALISTS

In the autumn of the year 1779 an English poet, writing in the seclusion of his garden at Olney, paid his respects to the American revolutionists in the following lines:

Yon roaring boys, who rave and fight On t'other side the Atlantic, I always held them in the right, But most so when most frantic.

When lawless mobs insult the court, That man shall be my toast, If breaking windows be the sport, Who bravely breaks the most.

But oh! for him my fancy culls The choicest flowers she bears, Who constitutionally pulls Your house about your ears.

When William Cowper wrote these lines, his sources of information with regard to affairs in America were probably slight; but had he been writing at the seat of war he could not have touched off the treatment of the Loyalists by the revolutionists with more effective irony.

There were two kinds of persecution to which the Loyalists were subjected-- that which was perpetrated by 'lawless mobs,' and that which was carried out 'constitutionally.'

It was at the hands of the mob that the Loyalists first suffered persecution. Probably the worst of the revolutionary mobs was that which paraded the streets of Boston. In 1765, at the time of the Stamp Act agitation, large crowds in Boston attacked and destroyed the magnificent houses of Andrew Oliver and Thomas Hutchinson. They broke down the doors with broadaxes, destroyed the furniture, stole the money and jewels, scattered the books and papers, and, having drunk the wines in the cellar, proceeded to the dismantling of the roof and walls. The owners of the houses barely escaped with their lives. In 1768 the same mob wantonly attacked the British troops in Boston, and so precipitated what American historians used to term 'the Boston Massacre'; and in 1773 the famous band of 'Boston Indians' threw the tea into Boston harbour.

In other places the excesses of the mob were nearly as great. In New York they were active in destroying printing-presses from which had issued Tory pamphlets, in breaking windows of private houses, in stealing live stock and personal effects, and in destroying property. A favourite pastime was tarring and feathering 'obnoxious Tories.' This consisted in stripping the victim naked, smearing him with a coat of tar and feathers, and parading him about the streets in a cart for the contemplation of his neighbours. Another amusement was making Tories ride the rail. This consisted in putting the 'unhappy victims upon sharp rails with one leg on each side; each rail was carried upon the shoulders of two tall men, with a man on each side to keep the poor wretch straight and fixed in his seat.'

Even clergymen were not free from the attentions of the mob. The Rev. Jonathan Boucher tells us that he was compelled to preach with loaded pistols placed on the pulpit cushions beside him. On one occasion he was prevented from entering the pulpit by two hundred armed men, whose leader warned him not to attempt to preach. 'I returned for answer,' says Boucher, 'that there was but one way by which they could keep me out of it, and that was by taking away my life. At the proper time, with my sermon in one hand and a loaded pistol in the other, like Nehemiah I prepared to ascend my pulpit, when one of my friends, Mr David Crauford, having got behind me, threw his arms round me and held me fast. He assured me that he had heard the most positive orders given to twenty men picked out for the purpose, to fire on me the moment I got into the pulpit.'

That the practices of the mob were not frowned upon by the revolutionary leaders, there is good reason for believing. The provincial Congress of New York, in December 1776, went so far as to order the committee of public safety to secure all the pitch and tar 'necessary for the public use and public safety.' Even Washington seems to have approved of persecution of the Tories by the mob. In 1776 General Putnam, meeting a procession of the Sons of Liberty who were parading a number of Tories on rails up and down the street's of New York, attempted to put a stop to the barbarous proceeding. Washington, on hearing of this, administered a reprimand to Putnam, declaring 'that to discourage such proceedings was to injure the cause of liberty in which they were engaged, and that nobody would attempt it but an enemy to his country.'

Very early in the Revolution the Whigs began to organize. They first formed themselves into local associations, similar to the Puritan associations in the Great Rebellion in England, and announced that they would 'hold all those persons inimical to the liberties of the colonies who shall refuse to subscribe this association.' In connection with these associations there sprang up local committees.

From garrets, cellars, rushing through the street, The new-born statesmen in committee meet,

sang a Loyalist verse-writer. Very soon there was completed an organization, stretching from the Continental Congress and the provincial congresses at one end down to the pettiest parish committees on the other, which was destined to prove a most effective engine for stamping out loyalism, and which was to contribute in no small degree to the success of the Revolution.

Though the action of the mob never entirely disappeared, the persecution of the Tories was taken over, as soon as the Revolution got under way, by this semi-official organization. What usually happened was that the Continental or provincial Congress laid down the general policy to be followed, and the local committees carried it out in detail. Thus, when early in 1776 the Continental Congress recommended the disarming of the Tories, it was the local committees which carried the recommendation into effect. During this early period the conduct of the revolutionary authorities was remarkably moderate. They arrested the Tories, tried them, held them at bail for their good behaviour, quarantined them in their houses, exiled them to other districts, but only in extreme cases did they imprison them. There was, of course, a good deal of hardship entailed on the Tories; and occasionally the agents of the revolutionary committees acted without authority, as when Colonel Dayton, who was sent to arrest Sir John Johnson at his home in the Mohawk valley, sacked Johnson Hall and carried off Lady Johnson a prisoner, on finding that Sir John Johnson had escaped to Canada with many of his Highland retainers. But, as a rule, in this early period, the measures taken both by the revolutionary committees and by the army officers were easily defensible on the ground of military necessity.

But with the Declaration of Independence a new order of things was inaugurated. That measure revolutionized the political situation. With the severance of the Imperial tie, loyalism became tantamount to treason to the state; and Loyalists laid themselves open to all the penalties of treason. The Declaration of Independence was followed by the test laws. These laws compelled every one to abjure allegiance to the British crown, and swear allegiance to the state in which he resided. A record was kept of those who took the oath, and to them were given certificates without which no traveller was safe from arrest. Those who failed to take the oath became liable to imprisonment, confiscation of property, banishment, and even death.

Even among the Whigs there was a good deal of opposition to the test laws. Peter Van Schaak, a moderate Whig of New York state, so strongly disapproved of the test laws that he seceded from the revolutionary party. 'Had you,' he wrote, 'at the beginning of the war, permitted every one differing in sentiment from you, to take the other side, or at least to have removed out of the State, with their property ... it would have been a conduct magnanimous and just. But, now, after restraining those persons from removing; punishing them, if, in the attempt, they were apprehended; selling their estates if they escaped; compelling them to the duties of subjects under heavy penalties; deriving aid from them in the prosecution of the war ... now to compel them to take an oath is an act of severity.'

Of course, the test laws were not rigidly or universally enforced. In Pennsylvania only a small proportion of the population took the oath. In New York, out of one thousand Tories arrested for failure to take the oath, six hundred were allowed to go on bail, and the rest were merely acquitted or imprisoned. On the whole the American revolutionists were not bloody-minded men; they inaugurated no September Massacres, no Reign of Terror, no dragonnades. There was a distinct aversion among them to applying the death penalty. 'We shall have many unhappy persons to take their trials for their life next Oyer court,' wrote a North Carolina patriot. 'Law should be strictly adhered to, severity exercised, but the doors of mercy should never be shut.'

The test laws, nevertheless, and the other discriminating laws passed against the Loyalists provided the excuse for a great deal of barbarism and ruthlessness. In Pennsylvania bills of attainder were passed against no fewer than four hundred and ninety persons. The property of nearly all these persons was confiscated, and several of them were put to death. A detailed account has come down to us of the hanging of two Loyalists of Philadelphia named Roberts and Carlisle. These two men had shown great zeal for the king's cause when the British Army was in Philadelphia. After Philadelphia was evacuated, they were seized by the Whigs, tried, and condemned to be hanged. Roberts's wife and children went before Congress and on their knees begged for mercy; but in vain. One November morning of 1778 the two men were marched to the gallows, with halters round their necks. At the gallows, wrote a spectator, Roberts's behaviour 'did honour to human nature.'

He nothing common did or mean Upon that memorable scene

Addressing the spectators, he told them that his conscience acquitted him of guilt; that he suffered for doing his duty to his sovereign; and that his blood would one day be required at their hands. Then he turned to his children and charged them to remember the principles for which he died, and to adhere to them while they had breath.

But if these judicial murders were few and far between, in other respects the revolutionists showed the Tories little mercy. Both those who remained in the country and those who fled from it were subjected to an attack on their personal fortunes which gradually impoverished them. This was carried on at first by a nibbling system of fines and special taxation. Loyalists were fined for evading military service, for the hire of substitutes, for any manifestation of loyalty. They were subjected to double and treble taxes; and in New York and South Carolina they had to make good all robberies committed in their counties. Then the revolutionary leaders turned to the expedient of confiscation. From the very first some of the patriots, without doubt, had an eye on Loyalist property; and when the coffers of the Continental Congress had been emptied, the idea gained ground that the Revolution might be financed by the confiscation of Loyalist estates. Late in 1777 the plan was embodied in a resolution of the Continental Congress, and the states were recommended to invest the proceeds in continental loan certificates. The idea proved very popular; and in spite of a great deal of corruption in connection with the sale and transfer of the land, large sums found their way as a result into the state exchequers. In New York alone over 3,600,000 pounds worth of property was acquired by the state.

The Tory who refused to take the oath of allegiance became in fact an outlaw. He did not have in the courts of law even the rights of a foreigner. If his neighbours owed him money, he had no legal redress. He might be assaulted, insulted, blackmailed, or slandered, yet the law granted him no remedy. No relative or friend could leave an orphan child to his guardianship. He could be the executor or administrator of no man's estate. He could neither buy land nor transfer it to another. If he was a lawyer, he was denied the right to practise his profession.

This strict legal view of the status of the Loyalist may not have been always and everywhere enforced. There were Loyalists, such as the Rev. Mather Byles of Boston, who refused to be molested, and who survived the Revolution unharmed. But when all allowance is made for these exceptions, it is not difficult to understand how the great majority of avowed Tories came to take refuge within the British lines, to enlist under the British flag, and, when the Revolution had proved successful, to leave their homes for ever and begin life anew amid other surroundings. The persecution to which they were subjected left them no alternative.

CHAPTER IV

THE LOYALISTS UNDER ARMS

It has been charged against the Loyalists, and the charge cannot be denied, that at the beginning of the Revolution they lacked initiative, and were slow to organize and defend themselves. It was not, in fact, until 1776 that Loyalist regiments began to be formed on an extensive scale. There were several reasons why this was so. In the first place a great many of the Loyalists, as has been pointed out, were not at the outset in complete sympathy with the policy of the British government; and those who might have been willing to take up arms were very early disarmed and intimidated by the energy of the revolutionary authorities. In the second place that very conservatism which made the Loyalists draw back from revolution hindered them from taking arms until the king gave them commissions and provided facilities for military organization. And there is no fact better attested in the history of the Revolution than the failure of the British authorities to understand until it was too late the great advantages to be derived from the employment of Loyalist levies. The truth is that the British officers did not think much more highly of the Loyalists than they did of the rebels. For both they had the Briton's contempt for the colonial, and the professional soldier's contempt for the armed civilian.

Had more use been made of the Tories, the military history of the Revolution might have been very different. They understood the conditions of warfare in the New World much better than the British regulars or the German mercenaries. Had the advice of prominent Loyalists been accepted by the British commander at the battle of Bunker's Hill, it is highly probable that there would have been none of that carnage in the British ranks which made of the victory a virtual defeat. It was said that Burgoyne's early successes were largely due to the skill with which he used his Loyalist auxiliaries. And in the latter part of the war, it must be confessed that the successes of the Loyalist troops far outshone those of the British regulars. In the Carolinas Tarleton's Loyal Cavalry swept everything before them, until their defeat at the Cowpens by Daniel Morgan. In southern New York Governor Tryon's levies carried fire and sword up the Hudson, into 'Indigo Connecticut,' and over into New Jersey. Along the northern frontier, the Loyalist forces commanded by Sir John Johnson and Colonel Butler made repeated incursions into the Mohawk, Schoharie, and Wyoming valleys and, in each case, after leaving a trail of desolation behind them, they withdrew to the Canadian border in good order. The trouble was that, owing to the stupidity and incapacity of Lord George Germain, the British minister who was more than any other man responsible for the misconduct of the American War, these expeditions were not made part of a properly concerted plan; and so they sank into the category of isolated raids.

From the point of view of Canadian history, the most interesting of these expeditions were those conducted by Sir John Johnson and Colonel Butler. They were carried on with the Canadian border as their base-line. It was by the men who were engaged in them that Upper Canada was at first largely settled; and for a century and a quarter there have been levelled against these men by American and even by English writers charges of barbarism and inhumanity about which Canadians in particular are interested to know the truth.

Most of Johnson's and Butler's men came from central or northern New York. To explain how this came about it is necessary to make an excursion into previous history. In 1738 there had come out to America a young Irishman of good family named William Johnson. The famous naval hero, Sir Peter Warren, who was an uncle of Johnson, had large tracts of land in the Mohawk valley, in northern New York. These estates he employed his nephew in administering; and, when he died, he bequeathed them to him. In the meantime William Johnson had begun to improve his opportunities. He had built up a prosperous trade with the Indians; he had learned their language and studied their ways; and he had gained such an ascendancy over them that he came to be known as 'the Indian-tamer,' and was appointed the British superintendent-general for Indian Affairs. In the Seven Years' War he served with great distinction against the French. He defeated Baron Dieskau at Lake George in 1755, and he captured Niagara in 1759; for the first of these services he was created a baronet, and received a pension of 5,000 pounds a year. During his later years he lived at his house, Johnson Hall, on the Mohawk river; and he died in 1774, on the eve of the American Revolution, leaving his title and his vast estates to his only son, Sir John.

Just before his death Sir William Johnson had interested himself in schemes for the colonization of his lands. In these he was remarkably successful. He secured in the main two classes of immigrants, Germans and Scottish Highlanders. Of the Highlanders he must have induced more than one thousand to emigrate from Scotland, some of them as late as 1773. Many of them had been Jacobites; some of them had seen service at Culloden Moor; and one of them, Alexander Macdonell, whose son subsequently sat in the first legislature of Upper Canada, had been on Bonnie Prince Charlie's personal staff. These men had no love for the Hanoverians; but their loyalty to their new chieftain, and their lack of sympathy with American ideals, kept them at the time of the Revolution true almost without exception to the British cause. King George had no more faithful allies in the New World than these rebels of the '45.

They were the first of the Loyalists to arm and organize themselves. In the summer of 1775 Colonel Allan Maclean, a Scottish officer in the English army, aided by Colonel Guy Johnson, a brother-in-law of Sir John Johnson, raised a regiment in the Mohawk valley known as the Royal Highland Emigrants, which he took to Canada, and which did good service against the American invaders under Montgomery in the autumn of the same year. In the spring of 1776 Sir John Johnson received word that the revolutionary authorities had determined on his arrest, and he was compelled to flee from Johnson Hall to Canada. With him he took three hundred of his Scottish dependants; and he was followed by the Mohawk Indians under their famous chief, Joseph Brant. In Canada Johnson received a colonel's commission to raise two Loyalist battalions of five hundred men each, to be known as the King's Royal Regiment of New York. The full complement was soon made up from the numbers of Loyalists who flocked across the border from other counties of northern New York; and Sir John Johnson's 'Royal Greens,' as they were commonly called, were in the thick of nearly every border foray from that time until the end of the war. It was by these men that the north shore of the St Lawrence river, between Montreal and Kingston, was mainly settled. As the tide of refugees swelled, other regiments were formed. Colonel John

Butler, one of Sir John Johnson's right-hand men, organized his Loyal Rangers, a body of irregular troops who adopted, with modifications, the Indian method of warfare. It was against this corps that some of the most serious charges of brutality and bloodthirstiness were made by American historians; and it was by this corps that the Niagara district of Upper Canada was settled after the war.

It is not possible here to give more than a brief sketch of the operations of these troops. In 1777 they formed an important part of the forces with which General Burgoyne, by way of Lake Champlain, and Colonel St Leger, by way of Oswego, attempted, unsuccessfully, to reach Albany. An offshoot of the first battalion of the 'Royal Greens,' known as Jessup's Corps, was with Burgoyne at Saratoga; and the rest of the regiment was with St Leger, under the command of Sir John Johnson himself. The ambuscade of Oriskany, where Sir John Johnson's men first met their Whig neighbours and relatives, who were defending Fort Stanwix, was one of the bloodiest battles of the war. Its 'fratricidal butchery' denuded the Mohawk valley of most of its male population; and it was said that if Tryon county 'smiled again during the war, it smiled through tears.' The battle was inconclusive, so bitterly was it contested; but it was successful in stemming the advance of St Leger's forces.

The next year (1778) there was an outbreak of sporadic raiding all along the border. Alexander Macdonell, the former aide-de-camp of Bonnie Prince Charlie, fell with three hundred Loyalists on the Dutch settlements of the Schoharie valley and laid them waste. Macdonell's ideas of border warfare were derived from his Highland ancestors; and, as he expected no quarter, he gave none. Colonel Butler, with his Rangers and a party of Indians, descended into the valley of Wyoming, which was a sort of debatable ground between Connecticut and Pennsylvania, and carried fire and sword through the settlements there. This raid was commemorated by Thomas Campbell in a most unhistorical poem entitled Gertrude of Wyoming:

On Susquehana's side, fair Wyoming! Although the wild-flower on thy ruined wall And roofless homes a sad remembrance bring Of what thy gentle people did befall.

Later in the year Walter Butler, the son of Colonel John Butler, and Joseph Brant, with a party of Loyalists and Mohawks, made a similar inroad on Cherry Valley, south of Springfield in the state of New York. On this occasion Brant's Indians got beyond control, and more than fifty defenceless old men, women, and children were slaughtered in cold blood.

The Americans took their revenge the following year. A large force under General Sullivan invaded the settlements of the Six Nations Indians in the Chemung and Genesee valleys, and exacted an eye for an eye and a tooth for a tooth. They burned the villages, destroyed the crops, and turned the helpless women and children out to face the coming winter. Most of the Indians during the winter of 1779-80 were dependent on the mercy of the British commissaries.

This kind of warfare tends to perpetuate itself indefinitely. In 1780 the Loyalists and Indians returned to the attack. In May Sir John Johnson with his 'Royal Greens' made a descent into the Mohawk valley, fell upon his 'rebellious birthplace,' and carried off rich booty and many prisoners. In the early autumn, with a force composed of his own regiment, two hundred of Butler's Rangers, and some regulars and Indians, he crossed over to the Schoharie valley, devastated it, and then returned to the Mohawk valley, where he completed the work of the previous spring. All attempts to crush him failed. At the battle of Fox's Mills he escaped defeat or capture by the American forces under General Van Rensselaer largely on account of the dense smoke with which the air was filled from the burning of barns and villages.

How far the Loyalists under Johnson and Butler were open to the charges of inhumanity and barbarism so often levelled against them, is difficult to determine. The charges are based almost wholly on unsubstantial tradition. The greater part of the excesses complained of, it is safe to say, were perpetrated by the Indians; and Sir John Johnson and Colonel Butler can no more be blamed for the excesses of the Indians at Cherry Valley than Montcalm can be blamed for their excesses at Fort William Henry. It was unfortunate that the military opinion of that day regarded the use of savages as necessary, and no one deplored this use more than men like Haldimand and Carleton; but Washington and the Continental Congress were as ready to receive the aid of the Indians as were the British. The difficulty of the Americans was that most of the Indians were on the other side.

That there were, however, atrocities committed by the Loyalists cannot be doubted. Sir John Johnson himself told the revolutionists that 'their Tory neighbours, and not himself, were blameable for those acts.' There are well-authenticated cases of atrocities committed by Alexander Macdonell: in 1781 he ordered his men to shoot down a prisoner taken near Johnstown, and when the men bungled their task, Macdonell cut the prisoner down with his broadsword. When Colonel Butler returned from Cherry Valley, Sir Frederick Haldimand refused to see him, and wrote to him that 'such indiscriminate vengeance taken even upon the treacherous and cruel enemy they are engaged against is useless and disreputable to themselves, as it is contrary to the disposition and maxims of their King whose cause they are fighting.'

But rumour exaggerated whatever atrocities there were. For many years the Americans believed that the Tories had lifted scalps like the Indians; and later, when the Americans captured York in 1813, they found what they regarded as a signal proof of this barbarous practice among the Loyalists, in the speaker's wig, which was hanging beside the chair in the legislative chamber! There may have been members of Butler's Rangers who borrowed from the Indians this hideous custom, just as there were American frontiersmen who were guilty of it; but it must not be imagined that it was a common practice on either side. Except at Cherry Valley, there is no proof that any violence was done by the Loyalists to women and children. On his return from Wyoming, Colonel Butler reported: 'I can with truth inform you that in the destruction of this settlement not a single person has been hurt of the inhabitants, but such as were armed; to those indeed the Indians gave no quarter.'

In defence of the Loyalists, two considerations may be urged. In the first place, it must be remembered that they were men who had been evicted from their homes, and whose property had been confiscated. They had been placed under the ban of the law: the payment of their debts had been denied them; and they had been forbidden to return to their native land under penalty of death without benefit of clergy. They had been imprisoned, fined, subjected to special taxation; their families had been maltreated, and were in many cases still in the hands of their enemies. They would have been hardly human had they waged a mimic warfare. In the second place, their depredations were of great value from a military point of view. Not only did they prevent thousands of militiamen from joining the Continental army, but they seriously threatened the sources of Washington's food supply. The valleys which they ravaged were the granary of the revolutionary forces. In 1780 Sir John Johnson destroyed in the Schoharie valley alone no less than eighty thousand bushels of grain; and this loss, as Washington wrote to the president of Congress, 'threatened alarming consequences.' That this work of destruction was agreeable to the Loyalists cannot be doubted; but this fact does not diminish its value as a military measure.

CHAPTER V

PEACE WITHOUT HONOUR

The war was brought to a virtual termination by the surrender of Cornwallis at Yorktown on October 19, 1781. The definitive articles of peace were signed at Versailles on September 3, 1783. During the two years that intervened between these events, the lot of the Loyalists was one of gloomy uncertainty. They found it hard to believe that the British government would abandon them to the mercy of their enemies; and yet the temper of the revolutionists toward them continued such that there seemed little hope of concession or conciliation. Success had not taught the rebels the grace of forgiveness. At the capitulation of Yorktown, Washington had refused to treat with the Loyalists in Cornwallis's army on the same terms as with the British regulars;

and Cornwallis had been compelled to smuggle his Loyalist levies out of Yorktown on the ship that carried the news of his surrender to New York. As late as 1782 fresh confiscation laws had been passed in Georgia and the Carolinas; and in New York a law had been passed cancelling all debts due to Loyalists, on condition that one-fortieth of the debt was paid into the state treasury. These were straws which showed the way the wind was blowing.

In the negotiations leading up to the Peace of Versailles there were no clauses so long and bitterly discussed as those relating to the Loyalists. The British commissioners stood out at first for the principle of complete amnesty to them and restitution of all they had lost; and it is noteworthy that the French minister added his plea to theirs. But Benjamin Franklin and his colleagues refused to agree to this formula. They took the ground that they, as the representatives merely of the Continental Congress, had not the right to bind the individual states in such a matter. The argument was a quibble. Their real reason was that they were well aware that public opinion in America would not support them in such a concession. A few enlightened men in America, such as John Adams, favoured a policy of compensation to the Loyalists, 'how little soever they deserve it, nay, how much soever they deserve the contrary'; but the attitude of the great majority of the Americans had been clearly demonstrated by a resolution passed in the legislature of Virginia on December 17, 1782, to the effect that all demands for the restitution of confiscated property were wholly inadmissible. Even some of the Loyalists had begun to realize that a revolution which had touched property was bound to be permanent, and that the American commissioners could no more give back to them their confiscated lands than Charles II was able to give back to his father's cavaliers the estates they had lost in the Civil War.

The American commissioners agreed, finally, that no future confiscations should take place, that imprisoned Loyalists should be released, that no further persecutions should be permitted, and that creditors on either side should 'meet with no lawful impediment' to the recovery of all good debts in sterling money. But with regard to the British demand for restitution, all they could be induced to sign was a promise that Congress would 'earnestly recommend to the legislatures of the respective states' a policy of amnesty and restitution.

In making this last recommendation, it is difficult not to convict the American commissioners of something very like hypocrisy. There seems to be no doubt that they knew the recommendation would not be complied with; and little or no attempt was made by them to persuade the states to comply with it. In after years the clause was represented by the Americans as a mere form of words, necessary to bring the negotiations to an end, and to save the face of the British government. To this day it has remained, except in one or two states, a dead letter. On the other hand it is impossible not to convict the British commissioners of a betrayal of the Loyalists. 'Never,' said Lord North in the House of Commons, 'never was the honour, the humanity, the principles, the policy of a nation so grossly abused, as in the desertion of those men who are now exposed to every punishment that desertion and poverty can inflict, because they were not rebels.' 'In ancient or in modern history,' said Lord Loughborough in the House of Lords, 'there cannot be found an instance of so shameful a desertion of men who have sacrificed all to their duty and to their reliance upon our faith.' It seems probable that the British commissioners could have obtained, on paper at any rate, better terms for the Loyalists. It is very doubtful if the Americans would have gone to war again over such a question. In 1783 the position of Great Britain was relatively not weaker, but stronger, than in 1781, when hostilities had ceased. The attitude of the French minister, and the state of the French finances, made it unlikely that France would lend her support to further hostilities. And there is no doubt that the American states were even more sorely in need of peace than was Great Britain.

When the terms of peace were announced, great was the bitterness among the Loyalists. One of them protested in Rivington's Gazette that 'even robbers, murderers, and rebels are faithful to their fellows and never betray each other,' and another sang,

'Tis an honour to serve the bravest of nations, And be left to be hanged in their capitulations.

If the terms of the peace had been observed, the plight of the Loyalists would have been bad enough. But as it was, the outcome proved even worse. Every clause in the treaty relating to the Loyalists was broken over and over again. There was no sign of an abatement of the popular feeling against them; indeed, in some places, the spirit of persecution seemed to blaze out anew. One of Washington's bitterest sayings was uttered at this time, when he said of the Loyalists that 'he could see nothing better for them than to commit suicide.' Loyalist creditors found it impossible to recover their debts in America, while they were themselves sued in the British courts by their American creditors, and their property was still being confiscated by the American legislatures. The legislature of New York publicly declined to reverse its policy of confiscation, on the ground that Great Britain had offered no compensation for the property which her friends had destroyed. Loyalists who ventured to return home under the treaty of peace were insulted, tarred and feathered, whipped, and even ham-strung. All over the country there were formed local committees or associations with the object of preventing renewed intercourse with the Loyalists and the restitution of Loyalist property. 'The proceedings of these people,' wrote Sir Guy Carleton, 'are not to be attributed to politics alone--it serves as a pretence, and under that cloak they act more boldly, but avarice and a desire of rapine are the great incentives.'

The Loyalists were even denied civil rights in most of the states. In 1784 an act was passed in New York declaring that all who had held office under the British, or helped to fit out vessels of war, or who had served as privates or officers in the British Army, or who had left the state, were guilty of 'misprision of treason,' and were disqualified from both the franchise and public office. There was in fact hardly a state in 1785 where the Loyalist was allowed to vote. In New York Loyalist lawyers were not allowed to practise until April 1786, and then only on condition of taking an 'oath of abjuration and allegiance.' In the same state, Loyalists were subjected to such invidious special taxation that in 1785 one of them confessed that 'those in New York whose estates have not been confiscated are so loaded with taxes and other grievances that there is nothing left but to sell out and move into the protection of the British government.'

It was clear that something would have to be done by the British government for the Loyalists' relief. 'It is utterly impossible,' wrote Sir Guy Carleton to Lord North, 'to leave exposed to the rage and violence of these people [the Americans] men of character whose only offence has been their attachment to the King's service.' Accordingly the British government made amends for its betrayal of the Loyalists by taking them under its wing. It arranged for the transportation of all those who wished to leave the revolted states; it offered them homes in the provinces of Nova Scotia and Quebec; it granted half-pay to the officers after their regiments were reduced; and it appointed a royal commission to provide compensation for the losses sustained.

CHAPTER VI

THE EXODUS TO NOVA SCOTIA

When the terms of peace became known, tens of thousands of the Loyalists shook the dust of their ungrateful country from their feet, never to return. Of these the more influential part, both during and after the war, sailed for England. The royal officials, the wealthy merchants, landowners, and professional men; the high military officers--these went to England to press their claims for compensation and preferment. The humbler element, for the most part, migrated to the remaining British colonies in North America. About two hundred families went to the West Indies, a few to Newfoundland, many to what were afterwards called Upper and Lower Canada, and a vast army to Nova Scotia, New Brunswick, and Prince Edward Island.

The advantages of Nova Scotia as a field for immigration had been known to the people of New England and New York before the Revolutionary War had broken out. Shortly after the Peace of 1763 parts of the Nova Scotian peninsula and the banks of the river St John had been sparsely settled by colonists from the south; and during the Revolutionary War considerable sympathy with the cause of the Continental Congress was shown by these colonists from New England. Nova Scotia, moreover, was contiguous to the New England colonies, and it was therefore not surprising that after the Revolution the Loyalists should have turned their eyes to Nova Scotia as a refuge for their families.

The first considerable migration took place at the time of the evacuation of Boston by General Howe in March 1776. Boston was at that time a town with a population of about sixteen thousand inhabitants, and of these nearly one thousand accompanied the British Army to Halifax. 'Neither Hell, Hull, nor Halifax,' said one of them, 'can afford worse shelter than Boston.' The embarkation was accomplished amid the most hopeless confusion. 'Nothing can be more diverting,' wrote a Whig, 'than to see the town in its present situation; all is uproar and confusion; carts, trucks, wheelbarrows, handbarrows, coaches, chaises, all driving as if the very devil was after them.' The fleet was composed of every vessel on which hands 'could be laid. In Benjamin Hallowell's cabin there were thirty-seven persons--men, women, and children; servants, masters, and mistresses--obliged to pig together on the floor, there being no berths.' It was a miracle that the crazy flotilla arrived safely at Halifax; but there it arrived after tossing about for six days in the March tempests. General Howe remained with his army at Halifax until June. Then he set sail for New York. Some of the Loyalists accompanied him to New York, but the greater number took passage for England. Only a few of the company remained in Nova Scotia.

From 1776 to 1783 small bodies of Loyalists continually found their way to Halifax; but it was not until the evacuation of New York by the British in 1783 that the full tide of immigration set in. As soon as news leaked out that the terms of peace were not likely to be favourable, and it became evident that the animus of the Whigs showed no signs of abating, the Loyalists gathered in New York looked about for a country in which to begin life anew. Most of them were too poor to think of going to England, and the British provinces to the north seemed the most hopeful place of resort. In 1782 several associations were formed in New York for the purpose of furthering the interests of those who proposed to settle in Nova Scotia. One of these associations had as its president the famous Dr Seabury, and as its secretary Sampson Salter Blowers, afterwards chief justice of Nova Scotia. Its officers waited on Sir Guy Carleton, and received his approval of their plans. It was arranged that a first instalment of about five hundred colonists should set out in the autumn of 1782, in charge of three agents, Amos Botsford, Samuel Cummings, and Frederick Hauser, whose duty it should be to spy out the land and obtain grants.

The party sailed from New York, in nine transport ships, on October 19, 1782, and arrived a few days later at Annapolis Royal. The population of Annapolis, which was only a little over a hundred, was soon swamped by the numbers that poured out of the transports. 'All the houses and barracks are crowded,' wrote the Rev. Jacob Bailey, who was then at Annapolis, 'and many are unable to procure any lodgings.' The three agents, leaving the colonists at Annapolis, went first to Halifax, and then set out on a trip of exploration through the Annapolis valley, after which they crossed the Bay of Fundy and explored the country adjacent to the river St John. On their return they published glowing accounts of the country, and their report was transmitted to their friends in New York.

The result of the favourable reports sent in by these agents, and by others who had gone ahead, was an invasion of Nova Scotia such as no one, not even the provincial authorities, had begun to expect. As the names of the thousands who were anxious to go to Nova Scotia poured into the adjutant-general's office in New York, it became clear to Sir Guy Carleton that with the shipping facilities at his disposal he could not attempt to transport them all at once. It was decided that the ships would have to make two trips; and, as a matter of fact, most of them made three or four trips before the last British soldier was able to leave the New York shore.

On April 26, 1783, the first or 'spring' fleet set sail. It had on board no less than seven thousand persons, men, women, children, and servants. Half of these went to the mouth of the river St John, and about half to Port Roseway, at the south-west end of the Nova Scotian peninsula. The voyage was fair, and the ships arrived at their destinations without mishap. But at St John at least, the colonists found that almost no preparations had been made to receive them. They were disembarked on a wild and primeval shore, where they had to clear away the brushwood before they could pitch their tents or build their shanties. The prospect must have been disheartening. 'Nothing but wilderness before our eyes, the women and children did not refrain from tears,' wrote one of the exiles; and the grandmother of Sir Leonard Tilley used to tell her descendants, 'I climbed to the top of Chipman's Hill and watched the sails disappearing in the distance, and such a feeling of loneliness came over me that, although I had not shed a tear through all the war, I sat down on the damp moss with my baby in my lap and cried.'

All summer and autumn the ships kept plying to and fro. In June the 'summer fleet' brought about 2,500 colonists to St John River, Annapolis, Port Roseway, and Fort Cumberland. By August 23 John Parr, the governor of Nova Scotia, wrote that 'upward of 12,000 souls have already arrived from New York,' and that as many more were expected. By the end of September he estimated that 18,000 had arrived, and stated that 10,000 more were still to come. By the end of the year he computed the total immigration to have amounted to 30,000. As late as January 15, 1784, the refugees were still arriving. On that date Governor Parr wrote to Lord North announcing the arrival of 'a considerable number of Refugee families, who must be provided for in and about the town at extraordinary expence, as at this season of the year I cannot send them into the country.' 'I cannot,' he added, 'better describe the wretched condition of these people than by inclosing your lordship a list of those just arrived in the Clinton transport, destitute of almost everything, chiefly women and children, all still on board, as I have not yet been able to find any sort of place for them, and the cold setting in severe.' There is a tradition in Halifax that the cabooses had to be taken off the ships, and ranged along the principal street, in order to shelter these unfortunates during the winter.

New York was evacuated by the British troops on November 25, 1783. Sir Guy Carleton did not withdraw from the city until he was satisfied that every person who desired the protection of the British flag was embarked on the boats. During the latter half of the year Carleton was repeatedly requested by Congress to fix some precise limit to his occupation of New York. He replied briefly, but courteously, that he was doing the best he could, and that no man could do more. When Congress objected that the Loyalists were not included in the agreement with regard to evacuation, Carleton replied that he held opposite views; and that in any case it was a point of honour with him that no troops should embark until the last person who claimed his protection should be safely on board a British ship. As time went on, his replies to Congress grew shorter and more incisive. On being requested to name an outside date for the evacuation of the city, he declared that he could not even guess when the last ship would be loaded, but that he was resolved to remain until it was. He pointed out, moreover, that the more the uncontrolled violence of their citizens drove refugees to his protection, the longer would evacuation be delayed. 'I should show,' he said, 'an indifference to the feelings of humanity, as well as to the honour and interest of the nation whom I serve, to leave any of the Loyalists that are desirous to quit the country, a prey to the violence they conceive they have so much cause to apprehend.'

After the evacuation of New York, therefore, the number of refugee Loyalists who came to Nova Scotia was small and insignificant. In 1784 and 1785 there arrived a few persons who had tried to take up the thread of their former life in the colonies, but had given up the attempt. And in August 1784 the Sally transport from London cast anchor at Halifax with three hundred destitute refugees on board. 'As if there was not a sufficiency of such distress'd objects already in this country,' wrote Edward Winslow from Halifax, 'the good people of England have collected a whole ship load of all kinds of vagrants from the streets of London, and sent them out to Nova Scotia. Great numbers died on the passage of various disorders--the miserable remnant are landed here and have now no covering but tents. Such as are able to crawl are begging for a proportion of provisions at my door.'

But the increase of population in Nova Scotia from immigration during the years immediately following 1783 was partly counterbalanced by the defections from the province. Many of the refugees quailed before the prospect of carving out a home in the wilderness. 'It is, I think, the roughest land I ever saw'; 'I am totally discouraged'; 'I am sick of this Province'--such expressions as these abound in the journals and diaries of the settlers. There were complaints that deception had been practised. 'All our golden promises,' wrote a Long Island Loyalist, 'are vanished in smoke. We were taught to believe this place was not barren and foggy as had been represented, but we find it ten times worse. We have nothing but his Majesty's rotten pork and unbaked flour to subsist on... It is the most inhospitable clime that ever mortal set foot on.' At first there was great distress among the refugees. The immigration of 1783 had at one stroke trebled the population of Nova Scotia; and the resources of the province were inadequate to meet the demand on them. 'Nova Scarcity' was the nickname for the province invented by a New England wit. Under these circumstances it is not surprising that some who had set their hand to the plough turned back. Some of them went to Upper Canada; some to England; some to the states from which they had come; for within a few years the fury of the anti-Loyalist feeling died down, and not a few Loyalists took advantage of this to return to the place of their birth.

The most careful analysis of the Loyalist immigration into the Maritime Provinces has placed the total number of immigrants at about 35,000. These were in settlements scattered broadcast over the face of the map. There was a colony of 3,000 in Cape Breton, which afforded an ideal field for settlement, since before 1783 the governor of Nova Scotia had been precluded from granting lands there. In 1784 Cape Breton was erected into a separate government, with a lieutenant-governor of its own; and settlers flocked into it from Halifax, and even from Canada. Abraham Cuyler, formerly mayor of Albany, led a considerable number down the St Lawrence and through the Gulf to Cape Breton. On the mainland of Nova Scotia there were settlements at Halifax, at Shelburne, at Fort Cumberland, at Annapolis and Digby; at Port Mouton, and at other places. In what is now New Brunswick there was a settlement at Passamaquoddy Bay, and there were other settlements on the St John river extending from the mouth up past what is now the city of Fredericton. In Prince Edward Island, then called the Island of St John, there was a settlement which is variously estimated in size, but which was comparatively unimportant.

The most interesting of these settlements was that at Shelburne, which is situated at the south-west corner of Nova Scotia, on one of the finest harbours of the Atlantic seaboard. The name of the harbour was originally Port Razoir, but this was corrupted by the English settlers into Port Roseway. The place had been settled previous to 1783. In 1775 Colonel Alexander McNutt, a notable figure of the pre-Loyalist days in Nova Scotia, had obtained a grant of 100,000 acres about the harbour, and had induced about a dozen Scottish and Irish families to settle there. This settlement he had dignified with the name of New Jerusalem. In a short time, however, New Jerusalem languished and died, and when the Loyalists arrived in May 1783, the only inhabitants of the place were two or three fishermen and their families. It would have been well if the Loyalists had listened to the testimony of one of these men, who, when he was asked how he came to be there, replied that 'poverty had brought him there, and poverty had kept him there.'

The project of settling the shores of Port Roseway had its birth in the autumn of 1782, when one hundred and twenty Loyalist families, whose attention had been directed to that part of Nova Scotia by a friend in Massachusetts, banded together with the object of emigrating thither. They first appointed a committee of seven to make arrangements for their removal; and, a few weeks later, they commissioned two members of the association, Joseph Pynchon and James Dole, to go to Halifax and lay before Governor Parr their desires and intentions. Pynchon and Dole, on their arrival at Halifax, had an interview with the governor, and obtained from him very satisfactory arrangements. The governor agreed to give the settlers the land about Port Roseway which they desired. He promised them that surveyors should be sent to lay out the grants, that carpenters and a supply of 400,000 feet of lumber should be furnished for building their houses, that for the first year at least the settlers should receive army rations, and that they should be free for ever from impressment in the British Navy. All these promises were made on the distinct understanding that they should interfere in no way with the claims of the Loyalists on the British government for compensation for losses sustained in the war. Elated by the reception they had received from the governor, the agents wrote home enthusiastic accounts of the prospects of the venture. Pynchon even hinted that the new town would supersede Halifax. 'Much talk is here,' he wrote, 'of capital of Province... Halifax can't but be sensible that Port Roseway, if properly attended to in encouraging settlers of every denomination, will have much the advantage of all supplies from the Bay of Fundy and westward. What the consequence will be time only will reveal.' Many persons at Halifax, wrote Pynchon, prophesied that the new settlement would dwindle, and recommended the shore of the Bay of Fundy or the banks of the river St John in preference to Port Roseway; but Pynchon attributed their fears to jealousy. A few years' experience must have convinced him that his suspicions were ill-founded.

The first instalment of settlers, about four thousand in number, arrived in May 1783. They found nothing but the virgin wilderness confronting them. But they set to work with a will to clear the land and build their houses. 'As soon as we had set up a kind of tent,' wrote the Rev. Jonathan Beecher in his Journal, 'we knelt down, my wife and I and my two boys, and kissed the dear ground and thanked God that the flag of England floated there, and resolved that we would work with the rest to become again prosperous and happy.' By July 11 the work of clearing had been so far advanced that it became possible to allot the lands. The town had been laid out in five long parallel streets, with other streets crossing them at right angles. Each associate was given a town lot fronting on one of these streets, as well as a water lot facing the harbour, and a fifty-acre farm in the surrounding country. With the aid of the government artisans, the wooden houses were rapidly run up; and in a couple of months a town sprang up where before had been the forest and some fishermen's huts.

At the end of July Governor Parr paid the town a visit, and christened it, curiously enough, with the name of Shelburne, after the British statesman who was responsible for the Peace of Versailles. The occasion was one of great ceremony. His Excellency, as he landed from the sloop Sophie, was saluted by the booming of cannon from the ships and from the shore. He proceeded up the main street, through a lane of armed men. At the place appointed for his reception he was met by the magistrates and principal citizens, and presented with an address. In the evening there was a dinner given by Captain Mowat on board the Sophie; and the next evening there was another dinner at the house of Justice Robertson, followed by a ball given by the citizens, which was 'conducted with the greatest festivity and decorum,' and 'did not break up till five the next morning.' Parr was delighted with Shelburne, and wrote to Sir Guy Carleton, 'From every appearance I have not a doubt but that it will in a short time become the most flourishing Town for trade of any in this part of the world, and the country will for agriculture.'

For a few years it looked as though Shelburne was not going to belie these hopes. The autumn of 1783 brought a considerable increase to its population; and in 1784 it seems to have numbered no less than ten thousand souls, including the suburb of Burchtown, in which most of the negro refugees in New York had been settled. It became a place of business and fashion. There was for a time an extensive trade in fish and lumber with Great Britain and the West Indies. Ship-yards were built, from which was launched the first ship built in Nova Scotia after the British occupation. Shops, taverns, churches, coffee-houses, sprang up. At one time no less than three newspapers were published in the town. The military were stationed there, and on summer evenings the military band played on the promenade near the bridge. On election day the main street was so crowded that 'one might have walked on the heads of the people.'

Then Shelburne fell into decay. It appeared that the region was ill-suited for farming and grazing, and was not capable of supporting so large a population. The whale fishery which the Shelburne merchants had established in Brazilian waters proved a failure. The regulations of the Navigation Acts thwarted their attempts to set up a coasting trade. Failure dogged all their enterprises, and soon the glory of Shelburne departed. It became like a city of the dead. 'The houses,' wrote Haliburton, 'were still standing though untenanted: It had all the stillness and quiet of a moonlight scene. It was difficult to imagine it was deserted. The idea of repose more readily suggested itself than decay. All was new and recent. Seclusion, and not death or removal, appeared to be the cause of the absence of inhabitants.' The same eye-witness of Shelburne's ruin described the town later:

The houses, which had been originally built of wood, had severally disappeared. Some had been taken to pieces and removed to Halifax or St John; others had been converted into fuel, and the rest had fallen a prey to neglect and decomposition. The chimneys stood up erect, and marked the spot around which the social circle had assembled; and the blackened fireplaces, ranged one above another, bespoke the size of the tenement and the means of its owner. In some places they had sunk with the edifice, leaving a heap of ruins, while not a few were inclining to their fall, and awaiting the first storm to repose again in the dust that now covered those who had constructed them. Hundreds of cellars with their stone walls and granite partitions were everywhere to be seen like uncovered monuments of the dead. Time and decay had done their work. All that was perishable had perished, and those numerous vaults spoke of a generation that had passed away for ever, and without the aid of an inscription, told a tale of sorrow and of sadness that overpowered the heart.

Alas for the dreams of the Pynchons and the Parrs! Shelburne is now a quaint and picturesque town; but it is not the city which its projectors planned.

CHAPTER VII

THE BIRTH OF NEW BRUNSWICK

When Governor Parr wrote to Sir Guy Carleton, commending in such warm terms the advantages of Shelburne, he took occasion at the same time to disparage the country about the river St John. 'I greatly fear,' he wrote, 'the soil and fertility of that part of this province is overrated by people who have explored it partially. I wish it may turn out otherwise, but have my fears that there is scarce good land enough for them already sent there.'

How Governor Parr came to make so egregious a mistake with regard to the comparative merits of the Shelburne districts and those of the St John river it is difficult to understand. Edward Winslow frankly accused him of jealousy of the St John settlements. Possibly he was only too well aware of the inadequacy of the preparations made to receive the Loyalists at the mouth of the St John, and wished to divert the stream of immigration elsewhere. At any rate his opinion was in direct conflict with the unanimous testimony of the agents sent to report on the land. Botsford, Cummings, and Hauser had reported: 'The St John is a fine river, equal in magnitude to the Connecticut or Hudson. At the mouth of the river is a fine harbour, accessible at all seasons of the year--never frozen or obstructed by ice... There are many settlers along the river upon the interval land, who get their living easily. The interval lies on the river, and is a most fertile soil, annually matured by the overflowing of the river, and produces crops of all kinds with little labour, and vegetables in the greatest perfection, parsnips of great length etc.' Later Lieutenant-Colonel Isaac Allen and Edward Winslow, the muster-master-general of the provincial forces, were sent up as agents for the Loyalist regiments in New York, and they explored the river for one hundred and twenty miles above its mouth. 'We have returned,' wrote Winslow after his trip, 'delighted beyond expression.'

Governor Parr's fears, therefore, had little effect on the popularity of the St John river district. In all, no less than ten thousand people settled on the north side of the Bay of Fundy in 1783. These came, in the main, in three divisions. With the spring fleet arrived about three thousand people; with the summer fleet not quite two thousand; and with the autumn fleet well over three thousand. Of those who came in the spring and summer most were civilian refugees; but of those who arrived in the autumn nearly all were disbanded soldiers. Altogether thirteen distinct corps settled on the St John river. There were the King's American Dragoons, De Lancey's First and Second Battalions, the New Jersey Volunteers, the King's American Regiment, the Maryland Loyalists, the 42nd Regiment, the Prince of Wales American Regiment, the New York Volunteers, the Royal Guides and Pioneers, the Queen's Rangers, the Pennsylvania Loyalists, and Arnold's American Legion. All these regiments were reduced, of course, to a fraction of their original strength, owing to the fact that numbers of their men had been discharged in New York, and that many of the officers had gone to England. But nevertheless, with their women and children, their numbers were not far from four thousand.

The arrangements which the government of Nova Scotia had made for the reception of this vast army of people were sadly inadequate. In the first place there was an unpardonable delay in the surveying and allotment of lands. This may be partly explained by the insufficient number of surveyors at the disposal of the governor, and by the tedious and difficult process of escheating lands already granted; but it is impossible not to convict the governor and his staff of want of foresight and expedition in making arrangements and carrying them into effect. When Joseph Aplin arrived at Parrtown, as the settlement at the mouth of the river was for a short time called, he found 1,500 frame houses and 400 log huts erected, but no one had yet received a title to the land on which his house was built. The case of the detachment of the King's American Dragoons who had settled near the mouth of the river was particularly hard. They had arrived in advance of the other troops, and had settled on the west side of the harbour of St John, in what Edward Winslow described as 'one of the pleasantest spots I ever beheld.' They had already made considerable improvements on their lands, when word came that the government had determined to reserve the lands about the mouth of the river for the refugees, and to allot blocks of land farther up the river to the various regiments of provincial troops. When news of this decision reached the officers of the provincial regiments, there was great indignation. 'This is so notorious a forfeiture of the faith of government,' wrote Colonel De Lancey to Edward Winslow, 'that it appears to me almost incredible, and yet I fear it is not to be doubted. Could we have known this a little earlier it would have saved you the trouble of exploring the country for the benefit of a people you are not connected with. In short it is a subject too disagreeable to say more upon.' Winslow, who was hot-headed, talked openly about the provincials defending the lands on which they had 'squatted.' But protests were in vain; and the King's American Dragoons were compelled to abandon their settlement, and to remove up the river to the district of Prince William. When the main body of the Loyalist regiments arrived in the autumn they found that the blocks of land assigned to them had not yet been surveyed. Of their distress and perplexity there is a picture in one of Edward Winslow's letters.

I saw [he says] all those Provincial Regiments, which we have so frequently mustered, landing in this inhospitable climate, in the month of October, without shelter, and without knowing where to find a place to reside. The chagrin of the officers was not to me so truly affecting as the poignant distress of the men. Those respectable sergeants of Robinson's, Ludlow's, Cruger's, Fanning's, etc.--once hospitable yeomen of the country--were addressing me in language which almost murdered me as I heard it. 'Sir, we have served all the war, your honour is witness how faithfully. We were promised land; we expected you had obtained it for us. We like the country--only let us have a spot of our own, and give us such kind of regulations as will hinder bad men from injuring us.'

Many of these men had ultimately to go up the river more than fifty miles past what is now Fredericton.

A second difficulty was that food and building materials supplied by government proved inadequate. At first the settlers were given lumber and bricks and tools to build their houses, but the later arrivals, who had as a rule to go farthest up the river, were compelled to find their building materials in the forest. Even the King's American Dragoons, evicted from their lands on the harbour of St John, were ordered to build their huts 'without any public expence.' Many were compelled to spend the winter in tents banked up with snow; others sheltered themselves in huts of bark. The privations and sufferings which many of the refugees suffered were piteous. Some, especially among the women and children, died from cold and exposure and insufficient food. In the third place there was great inequality in the area of the lands allotted. When the first refugees arrived, it was not expected that so many more would follow; and consequently the earlier grants were much larger in size than the later. In Parrtown a town lot at length shrank in size to one-sixteenth of what it had originally been. There was doubtless also some favouritism and respect of persons in the granting of lands. At any rate the inequality of the grants caused a great many grievances among a certain class of refugees. Chief Justice Finucane of Nova Scotia was sent by Governor Parr to attempt to smooth matters out; but his conduct seemed to accentuate the ill-feeling and alienate from the Nova Scotia authorities the good-will of some of the better class of Loyalists.

It was not surprising, under these circumstances, that Governor Parr and the officers of his government should have become very unpopular on the north side of the Bay of Fundy. Governor Parr was himself much distressed over the ill-feeling against him among the Loyalists; and it should be explained that his failure to satisfy them did not arise from unwillingness to do anything in his power to make them comfortable. The trouble was that his executive ability had not been sufficient to cope with the serious problems confronting him. Out of the feeling against Governor Parr arose an agitation to have the country north of the Bay of Fundy removed from his jurisdiction altogether, and erected into a separate government. This idea of the division of the province had been suggested by Edward Winslow as early as July 1783: 'Think what multitudes have and will come here, and then judge whether it must not from the nature of things immediately become a separate government.' There were good reasons why such a change should be made. The distance of Parrtown from Halifax made it very difficult and tedious to transact business with the government.' and the Halifax authorities, being old inhabitants, were not in complete sympathy with the new settlers. The erection of a new province, moreover, would provide offices for many of the Loyalists who were pressing their claims for place on the government at home. The settlers, therefore, brought their influence to bear on the Imperial authorities, through their friends in London; and in the summer of 1784 they succeeded in effecting the division they desired, in spite of the opposition of Governor Parr and the official class at Halifax. Governor Parr, indeed, had a narrow escape from being recalled.

The new province, which it was intended at first to call New Ireland, but which was eventually called New Brunswick, was to include all that part of Nova Scotia north of a line running across the isthmus from the mouth of the Missiquash river to its source, and thence across to the nearest part of Baie Verte. This boundary was another triumph for the Loyalists, as it placed in New Brunswick Fort Cumberland and the greater part of Cumberland county. The government of the province was offered first to General Fox, who had been in command at Halifax in 1783, and then to General Musgrave; but was declined by both. It was eventually accepted by Colonel Thomas Carleton, a brother of Sir Guy Carleton, by whom it was held for over thirty years. The chief offices of government fell to Loyalists who were in London. The secretary of the province was the Rev. Jonathan Odell, a witty New Jersey divine, who had been secretary to Sir Guy Carleton in New York. It is interesting to note that Odell's son, the Hon. W. F. Odell, was secretary of the province after him, and that between them they held the office for two-thirds of a century. The chief justice was a former judge of the Supreme Court of New York; the other judges were retired officers of regiments who had fought in the war. The attorney-general was Jonathan Bliss, of Massachusetts; and the solicitor-general was Ward Chipman, the friend and correspondent of Edward Winslow. Winslow himself, whose charming letters throw such a flood of light on the settlement of Nova Scotia and New Brunswick, was a member of the council. New Brunswick was indeed par excellence the Loyalist province.

The new governor arrived at Parrtown on November 21, 1784, and was immediately presented with an enthusiastic address of welcome by the inhabitants. They described themselves as 'a number of oppressed and insulted Loyalists,' and added that they had formerly been freemen, and again hoped to be so under his government. Next spring the governor granted to Parrtown incorporation as a city under the name of St John. The name Parrtown had been given, it appears, at the request of Governor Parr himself, who explained apologetically that the suggestion had arisen out of 'female vanity'; and in view of Governor Parr's unpopularity, the change of name was very welcome. At the same time, however, Colonel Carleton greatly offended the people of St John by removing the capital of the province up the river to St Anne's, to which he gave the name Fredericktown (Fredericton) in honour of the Duke of York.

On October 15, 1785, writs were issued for the election of members to serve in a general assembly. The province was divided into eight counties, among which were apportioned twenty-six members. The right to vote was given by Governor Carleton to all males of twenty-one years of age who had been three months in the province, the object of this very democratic franchise being to include in the voting list settlers who were clearing their lands, but had not yet received their grants. The elections were held in November, and lasted for fifteen days. They passed off without incident, except in the city of St John. There a struggle took place which throws a great deal of light on the bitterness of social feeling among the Loyalists. The inhabitants split into two parties, known as the Upper Cove and the Lower Cove. The Upper Cove represented the aristocratic element, and the Lower Cove the democratic. For some time class feeling had been growing; it had been aroused by the attempt of fifty-five gentlemen of New York to obtain for themselves, on account of their social standing and services during the war, grants of land in Nova Scotia of five thousand acres each; and it had been fanned into flame by the inequality in the size of the lots granted in St John itself. Unfortunately, among the six Upper Cove candidates in St John there were two officers of the government, Jonathan Bliss and Ward Chipman; and thus the struggle took on the appearance of one between government and opposition candidates. The election was bitterly contested, under the old method of open voting; and as it proceeded it became clear that the Lower Cove was polling a majority of the votes. The defeat of the government officers, it was felt, would be such a calamity that at the scrutiny Sheriff Oliver struck off over eighty votes, and returned the Upper Cove candidates. The election was protested, but the House of Assembly refused, on a technicality, to upset the election. A strangely ill-worded and ungrammatical petition to have the assembly dissolved was presented to the governor by the Lower Cove people, but Governor Carleton refused to interfere, and the Upper Cove candidates kept their seats. The incident created a great deal of indignation in St John, and Ward Chipman and Jonathan Bliss were not able for many years to obtain a majority in that riding.

It is evident from these early records that, while there were members of the oldest and most famous families in British America among the Loyalists of the Thirteen Colonies, the majority of those who came to Nova Scotia, New Brunswick, and especially to Upper Canada, were people of very humble origin. Of the settlers in Nova Scotia, Governor Parr expressed his regret 'that there is not a sufficient proportion of men of education and abilities among the present adventurers.' The election in St John was a sufficient evidence of the strength of the democratic element there; and their petition to Governor Carleton is a sufficient evidence of their illiteracy. Some of the settlers assumed pretensions to which they were not entitled. An amusing case is that of William Newton. This man had been the groom of the Honourable George Hanger, a major in the British Legion during the war. Having come to Nova Scotia, he began to pay court to a wealthy widow, and introduced himself to her by affirming 'that he was particularly connected with the hono'ble Major Hanger, and that his circumstances were rather affluent, having served in a money-making department, and that he had left a considerable property behind him.' The widow applied to Edward Winslow, who assured her that Mr Newton had indeed been connected--very closely-- with the Honourable Major Hanger, and that he had left a large property behind him. 'The nuptials were immediately celebrated with great pomp, and Mr Newton is at present,' wrote Winslow, 'a gentleman of consideration in Nova Scotia.'

During 1785 and subsequent years, the work of settlement went on rapidly in New Brunswick. There was hardship and privation at first, and up to 1792 some indigent settlers received rations from the government. But astonishing progress was made. 'The new settlements of the Loyalists,' wrote Colonel Thomas Dundas, who visited New Brunswick in the winter of 1786-87, 'are in a thriving way.' Apparently, however, he did not think highly of the industry of the disbanded soldiers, for he avowed that 'rum and idle habits contracted during the war are much against them.' But he paid a compliment to the half-pay officers. 'The half-pay provincial officers,' he wrote, 'are valuable settlers, as they are enabled to live well and improve their lands.'

It took some time for the province to settle down. Many who found their lands disappointing moved to other parts of the province; and after 1790 numbers went to Upper Canada. But gradually the settlers adjusted themselves to their environment, and New Brunswick entered on that era of prosperity which has been hers ever since.

CHAPTER VIII

IN PRINCE EDWARD ISLAND

Not many Loyalists found their way to Prince Edward Island, or, as it was called at the time of the American Revolution, the Island of St John. Probably there were not many more than six hundred on the island at any one time. But the story of these immigrants forms a chapter in itself. Elsewhere the refugees were well and loyally treated. In Nova Scotia and Quebec the English officials strove to the best of their ability, which was perhaps not always great, to make provision for them. But in Prince Edward Island they were the victims of treachery and duplicity.

Prince Edward Island was in 1783 owned by a number of large landed proprietors. When it became known that the British government intended to settle the Loyalists in Nova Scotia, these proprietors presented a petition to Lord North, declaring their desire to afford asylum to such as would settle on the island. To this end they offered to resign certain of their lands for colonization, on condition that the government abated the quit-rents. This petition was favourably received by the government, and a proclamation was issued promising lands to settlers in Prince Edward Island on terms similar to those granted to settlers in Nova Scotia and Quebec.

Encouraged by the liberal terms held forth, a number of Loyalists went to the island direct from New York, and a number went later from Shelburne, disappointed by the prospects there. In June 1784 a muster of Loyalists on the island was taken, which showed a total of about three hundred and eighty persons, and during the remainder of the year a couple of hundred went from Shelburne. At the end of 1784, therefore, it is safe to assume that there were nearly six hundred on the island, or about one-fifth of the total population.

These refugees found great difficulty in obtaining the grants of land promised to them. They were allowed to take up their residence on certain lands, being assured that their titles were secure; and then, after they had cleared the lands, erected buildings, planted orchards, and made other improvements, they were told that their titles lacked validity, and they were forced to move. Written title-deeds were withheld on every possible pretext, and when they were granted they were found to contain onerous conditions out of harmony with the promises made. The object of the proprietors, in inflicting these persecutions, seems to have been to force the settlers to become tenants instead of freeholders. Even Colonel Edmund Fanning, the Loyalist lieutenant-governor, was implicated in this conspiracy. Fanning was one of the proprietors in Township No. 50. The settlers in this township, being unable to obtain their grants, resolved to send a remonstrance to the British government, and chose as their representative one of their number who had known Lord Cornwallis during the war, hoping through him to obtain redress. This agent was on the point of leaving for England, when news of his intention reached Colonel Fanning. The ensuing result was as prompt as it was significant: within a week afterwards nearly all the Loyalists in Township No. 50 had obtained their grants.

Others, however, did not have friends in high places, and were unable to obtain redress. The minutes of council which contained the records of many of the allotments were not entered in the regular Council Book, but were kept on loose sheets; and thus the unfortunate settlers were not able to prove by the Council Book that their lands had been allotted them. When the rough minutes were discovered years later, they were found to bear evidence, in erasures and the use of different inks, of having been tampered with.

For seventy-five years the Loyalists continued to agitate for justice. As early as 1790 the island legislature passed an act empowering the governor to give grants to those who had not yet received them from the proprietors. But this measure did not entirely redress the grievances, and after a lapse of fifty years a petition of the descendants of the Loyalists led to further action in the matter. In 1840 a bill was passed by the House of Assembly granting relief to the Loyalists, but was thrown out by the Legislative Council. As late as 1860 the question was still troubling the island politics. In that year a land commission was appointed, which reported that there were Loyalists who still had claims on the local government, and recommended that free grants should be made to such as could prove that their fathers had been attracted to the island under promises which had never been fulfilled.

Such is the unlovely story of how the Loyalists were persecuted in the Island of St John, under the British flag.

CHAPTER IX

THE LOYALISTS IN QUEBEC

It was a tribute to the stability of British rule in the newly-won province of Quebec that at the very beginning of the Revolutionary War loyal refugees began to flock across the border. As early as June 2, 1774, Colonel Christie, stationed at St Johns on the Richelieu, wrote to Sir Frederick Haldimand at Quebec notifying him of the arrival of immigrants; and it is interesting to note that at that early date he already complained of 'their unreasonable expectations.' In the years 1775 and 1776 large bodies of persecuted Loyalists from the Mohawk valley came north with Sir John Johnson and Colonel Butler; and in these years was formed in Canada the first of the Loyalist regiments. It was not, however, until the defeat of Burgoyne at Saratoga in 1778 that the full tide of immigration set in. Immediately thereafter Haldimand wrote to Lord George Germain, under date of October 14, 1778, reporting the arrival of 'loyalists in great distress,' seeking refuge from the revolted provinces. Haldimand lost no time in making provision for their reception. He established a settlement for them at Machiche, near Three Rivers, which he placed under the superintendence of a compatriot and a protege of his named Conrad Gugy. The captains of militia in the neighbourhood were ordered to help build barracks for the refugees, provisions were secured from the merchants at Three Rivers, and everything in reason was done to make the unfortunates comfortable. By the autumn of 1778 there were in Canada, at Machiche and other places, more than one thousand refugees, men, women, and children, exclusive of those who had enlisted in the regiments. Including the troops, probably no less than three thousand had found their way to Canada.

With the conclusion of peace came a great rush to the north. The resources of government were strained to the utmost to provide for the necessities of the thousands who flocked over the border-line. At Chambly, St Johns, Montreal, Sorel, Machiche, Quebec, officers of government were stationed to dole out supplies. At Quebec alone in March 1784 one thousand three hundred and thirty-eight 'friends of government' were being fed at the public expense. At Sorel a settlement was established similar to that at Machiche. The seigneury of Sorel had been purchased by the government in 1780 for military purposes, and when the war was over it was turned into a Loyalist reserve, on which huts were erected and provisions dispensed. In all, there must have been nearly seven thousand Loyalists in the province of Quebec in the winter of 1783-84.

Complete details are lacking with regard to the temporary encampments in which the Loyalists were hived; but there are evidences that they were not entirely satisfied with the manner in which they were looked after. One of the earliest of Canadian county histories, [Footnote: Dundas, or a Sketch of Canadian History, by James Croil, Montreal, 1861.] a book partly based on traditionary sources, has some vague tales about the cruelty and malversation practised by a Frenchman under whom the Loyalists were placed at 'Mishish.' 'Mishish' is obviously a phonetic spelling of Machiche, and 'the Frenchman' is probably Conrad Gugy. Some letters in the Dominion Archives point in the same direction. Under date of April 29, the governor's secretary writes to Stephen De Lancey, the inspector of the Loyalists, referring to 'the uniform discontent of the Loyalists at Machiche.' The discontent, he explains, is excited by a few ill-disposed persons. 'The sickness they complain of has been common throughout the province, and should have lessened rather than increased the consumption of provisions.' A Loyalist who writes to the governor, putting his complaints on paper, is assured that 'His Excellency is anxious to do everything in his power for the Loyalists, but if what he can do does not come up to the expectation of him and those he represents, His Excellency gives the fullest permission to them to seek redress in such manner as they shall think best.'

What degree of justice there was in the complaints of the refugees it is now difficult to determine. No doubt some of them were confirmed grumblers, and many of them had what Colonel Christie called 'unreasonable expectations.' Nothing is more certain than that Sir Frederick Haldimand spared no effort to accommodate the Loyalists. On the other hand, it would be rash to assert that in the confusion which then reigned there were no grievances of which they could justly complain.

In the spring and summer of 1784 the great majority of the refugees within the limits of the province of Quebec were removed to what was afterwards known as Upper Canada. But some remained, and swelled the number of the 'old subjects' in the French province. Considerable settlements were made at two places. One of these was Sorel, where the seigneury that had been bought by the crown was granted out to the new-comers in lots; the other was in the Gaspe peninsula, on the shores of the Gulf of St Lawrence and of

Chaleur Bay. The seigneury of Sorel was well peopled, for each grantee received only sixty acres and a town lot, taking the rest of his allotment in some of the newer settlements. The settlement in the Gaspe peninsula was more sparse; the chief centre of population was the tiny fishing village of Paspebiac. In addition to these settlements, some of the exiles took up land on private seigneuries; these, however, were not many, for the government discouraged the practice, and refused supplies to all who did not settle on the king's land. At the present time, of all these Loyalist groups in the province of Quebec scarce a trace remains: they have all been swallowed up in the surrounding French population.

The Eastern Townships in the province of Quebec were not settled by the United Empire Loyalists. In 1783 Sir Frederick Haldimand set his face like flint against any attempt on the part of the Loyalists to settle the lands lying along the Vermont frontier. He feared that a settlement there would prove a permanent thorn in the flesh of the Americans, and might lead to much trouble and friction. He wished that these lands should be left unsettled for a time, and that, in the end, they should be settled by French Canadians 'as an antidote to the restless New England population.' Some of the more daring Loyalists, in spite of the prohibition of the governor, ventured to settle on Missisquoi Bay. When the governor heard of it, he sent orders to the officer commanding at St Johns that they should be removed as soon as the season should admit of it; and instructions were given that if any other Loyalists settled there, their houses were to be destroyed. By these drastic means the government kept the Eastern Townships a wilderness until after 1791, when the townships were granted out in free and common socage, and American settlers began to flock in. But, as will be explained, these later settlers have no just claim to the appellation of United Empire Loyalists.

CHAPTER X

THE WESTERN SETTLEMENTS

Sir Frederick Haldimand Offered the Loyalists a wide choice of places in which to settle. He was willing to make land grants on Chaleur Bay, at Gaspe, on the north shore of the St Lawrence above Montreal, on the Bay of Quinte, at Niagara, or along the Detroit river; and if none of these places was suitable, he offered to transport to Nova Scotia or Cape Breton those who wished to go thither. At all these places settlements of Loyalists sprang up. That at Niagara grew to considerable importance, and became after the division of the province in 1791 the capital of Upper Canada. But by far the largest settlement was that which Haldimand planned along the north shore of the St Lawrence and Lake Ontario between the western boundary of the government of Quebec and Cataraqui (now Kingston), east of the Bay of Quinte. Here the great majority of the Loyalists in Canada were concentrated.

As soon as Haldimand received instructions from England with regard to the granting of the lands he gave orders to Major Samuel Holland, surveyor-general of the king's territories in North America, to proceed with the work of making the necessary surveys. Major Holland, taking with him as assistants Lieutenants Kotte and Sutherland and deputy-surveyors John Collins and Patrick McNish, set out in the early autumn of 1783, and before the winter closed in he had completed the survey of five townships bordering on the Bay of Quinte. The next spring his men returned, and surveyed eight townships along the north bank of the St Lawrence, between the Bay of Quinte and the provincial boundary. These townships are now distinguished by names, but in 1783-84 they were designated merely by numbers; thus for many years the old inhabitants referred to the townships of Osnaburg, Williamsburg, and Matilda, for instance, as the 'third town,' the 'fourth town,' and the 'fifth town.' The surveys were made in great haste, and, it is to be feared, not with great care; for some tedious lawsuits arose out of the discrepancies contained in them, and a generation later Robert Gourlay wrote that 'one of the present surveyors informed me that in running new lines over a great extent of the province, he found spare room for a whole township in the midst of those laid out at an early period.' Each township was subdivided into lots of two hundred acres each, and a town-site was selected in each case which was subdivided into town lots.

The task of transporting the settlers from their camping-places at Sorel, Machiche, and St Johns to their new homes up the St Lawrence was one of some magnitude. General Haldimand was not able himself to oversee the work; but he appointed Sir John Johnson as superintendent, and the work of settlement went on under Johnson's care. On a given day the Loyalists were ordered to strike camp, and proceed in a body to the new settlements. Any who remained behind without sufficient excuse had their rations stopped. Bateaux took the settlers up the St Lawrence, and the various detachments were disembarked at their respective destinations. It had been decided that the settlers should be placed on the land as far as possible according to the corps in which they had served during the war, and that care should be taken to have the Protestant and Roman Catholic members of a corps settled separately. It was this arrangement which brought about the grouping of Protestant and Roman Catholic Scottish Highlanders in Glengarry. The first battalion of the King's Royal Regiment of New York was settled on the first five townships west of the provincial boundary. This was Sir John Johnson's regiment, and most of its members were his Scottish dependants from the Mohawk valley. The next three townships were settled by part of Jessup's Corps, an offshoot of Sir John Johnson's regiment. Of the Cataraqui townships the first was settled by a band of New York Loyalists, many of them of Dutch or German extraction, commanded by Captain Michael Grass. On the second were part of Jessup's Corps; on the third and fourth were a detachment of the second battalion of the King's Royal Regiment of New York, which had been stationed at Oswego across the lake at the close of the war, a detachment of Rogers's Rangers, and a party of New York Loyalists under Major Van Alstine. The parties commanded by Grass and Van Alstine had come by ship from New York to Quebec after the evacuation of New York in 1783. On the fifth township were various detachments of disbanded regular troops, and even a handful of disbanded German mercenaries.

As soon as the settlers had been placed on the townships to which they had been assigned, they received their allotments of land. The surveyor was the land agent, and the allotments were apportioned by each applicant drawing a lot out of a hat. This democratic method of allotting lands roused the indignation of some of the officers who had settled with their men. They felt that they should have been given the front lots, unmindful of the fact that their grants as officers were from five to ten times as large as the grants which their men received. Their protests, contained in a letter of Captain Grass to the governor, roused Haldimand to a display of warmth to which he was as a rule a stranger. Captain Grass and his associates, he wrote, were to get no special privileges, 'the most of them who came into the province with him being, in fact, mechanics, only removed from one situation to practise their trade in another. Mr Grass should, therefore, think himself very well off to draw lots in common with the Loyalists.' A good deal of difficulty arose also from the fact that many allotments were inferior to the rest from an agricultural point of view; but difficulties of this sort were adjusted by Johnson and Holland on the spot.

By 1784 nearly all the settlers were destitute and completely dependent on the generosity of the British government. They had no effects; they had no money; and in many cases they were sorely in need of clothes. The way in which Sir Frederick Haldimand came to their relief is deserving of high praise. If he had adhered to the letter of his instructions from England, the position of the Loyalists would have been a most unenviable one. Repeatedly, however, Haldimand took on his own shoulders the responsibility of ignoring or disobeying the instructions from England, and trusted to chance that his protests would prevent the government from repudiating his actions. When the home government, for instance, ordered a reduction of the rations, Haldimand undertook to continue them in full; and fortunately for him the home government, on receipt of his protest, rescinded the order.

The settlers on the Upper St Lawrence and the Bay of Quinte did not perhaps fare as well as those in Nova Scotia, or even the Mohawk Indians who settled on the Grand river. They did not receive lumber for building purposes, and 'bricks for the inside of their chimneys, and a little assistance of nails,' as did the former; nor did they receive ploughs and church-bells, as did the latter. For building lumber they had to wait until saw-mills were constructed; instead of ploughs they had at first to use hoes and spades, and there were not quite enough hoes and spades to go round. Still, they did not fare badly. When the difficulty of transporting things up the St Lawrence is remembered, it is remarkable that they obtained as much as they did. In the first place they were supplied with clothes for three years, or until they were able to provide clothes for themselves. These consisted of coarse cloth for trousers and Indian blankets for coats. Boots they made out of skins or heavy cloth. Tools for building were given them: to each family were given an ax and a hand-saw, though unfortunately the axes were short-handled ship's axes, ill-adapted to cutting in the forest; to each group of two families were allotted a whip-saw and a cross-cut saw; and to each group of five families was supplied a set of tools, containing chisels, augers, draw-knives, etc. To each group of five families was also allotted 'one fire-lock ... intended for the messes, the pigeon and wildfowl season'; but later on a fire-lock was supplied to every head of a family. Haldimand went to great trouble in obtaining seed-wheat for the settlers, sending agents down even into Vermont and the Mohawk valley to obtain all that was to be had; he declined, however, to supply stock for the farms, and although eventually he obtained some cattle, there were not nearly enough cows to go round. In many cases the soldiers were allowed the loan of the military tents; and everything was done to have saw-mills and grist-mills erected in the most convenient places with the greatest possible dispatch. In the meantime small portable grist-mills, worked by hand, were distributed among the settlers.

Among the papers relating to the Loyalists in the Canadian Archives there is an abstract of the numbers of the settlers in the five townships at Cataraqui and the eight townships on the St Lawrence. There were altogether 1,568 men, 626 women, 1,492 children, and 90 servants, making a total of 3,776 persons. These were, of course, only the original settlers. As time went on others were added. Many of the soldiers had left their families in the States behind them, and these families now hastened to cross the border. A proclamation had been issued by the British government inviting those Loyalists who still remained in the States to assemble at certain places along the frontier, namely, at Isle aux Noix, at Sackett's Harbour, at Oswego, and at Niagara. The favourite route was the old trail from the Mohawk valley to

Oswego, where was stationed a detachment of the 34th regiment. From Oswego these refugees crossed to Cataraqui. 'Loyalists,' wrote an officer at Cataraqui in the summer of 1784, 'are coming in daily across the lake.' To accommodate these new settlers three more townships had to be mapped out at the west end of the Bay of Quinte.

For the first few years the Cataraqui settlers had a severe struggle for existence. Most of them arrived in 1784, too late to attempt to sow fall wheat; and it was several seasons before their crops became nearly adequate for food. The difficulties of transportation up the St Lawrence rendered the arrival of supplies irregular and uncertain. Cut off as they were from civilization by the St Lawrence rapids, they were in a much less advantageous position than the great majority of the Nova Scotia and New Brunswick settlers, who were situated near the sea-coast. They had no money, and as the government refused to send them specie, they were compelled to fall back on barter as a means of trade, with the result that all trade was local and trivial. In the autumn of 1787 the crops failed, and in 1788 famine stalked through the land. There are many legends about what was known as 'the hungry year.' If we are to believe local tradition, some of the settlers actually died of starvation. In the family papers of one family is to be found a story about an old couple who were saved from starvation only by the pigeons which they were able to knock over. A member of another family testifies: 'We had the luxury of a cow which the family brought with them, and had it not been for this domestic boon, all would have perished in the year of scarcity.' Two hundred acre lots were sold for a few pounds of flour. A valuable cow, in one case, was sold for eight bushels of potatoes; a three-year-old horse was exchanged for half a hundredweight of flour. Bran was used for making cakes; and leeks, buds of trees, and even leaves, were ground into food.

The summer of 1789, however, brought relief to the settlers, and though, for many years, comforts and even necessaries were scarce, yet after 1791, the year in which the new settlements were erected into the province of Upper Canada, it may be said that most of the settlers had been placed on their feet. The soil was fruitful; communication and transportation improved; and metallic currency gradually found its way into the settlements. When Mrs Simcoe, the wife of the lieutenant-governor, passed through the country in 1792, she was struck by the neatness of the farms of the Dutch and German settlers from the Mohawk valley, and by the high quality of the wheat. 'I observed on my way thither,' she says in her diary, 'that the wheat appeared finer than any I have seen in England, and totally free from weeds.' And a few months later an anonymous English traveller, passing the same way, wrote: 'In so infant a settlement, it would have been irrational to expect that abundance which bursts the granaries, and lows in the stalls of more cultivated countries. There was, however, that kind of appearance which indicated that with economy and industry, there would be enough.'

Next in size to the settlements at Cataraqui and on the Upper St Lawrence was the settlement at Niagara. During the war Niagara had been a haven of refuge for the Loyalists of Pennsylvania and the frontier districts, just as Oswego and St Johns had been havens of refuge for the Loyalists of northern and western New York. As early as 1776 there arrived at Fort George, Niagara, in a starving condition, five women and thirty-six children, bearing names which are still to be found in the Niagara peninsula. From that date until the end of the war refugees continued to come in. Many of these refugees were the families of the men and officers of the Loyalist troops stationed at Niagara. On September 27, 1783, for instance, the officer commanding at Niagara reports the arrival from Schenectady of the wives of two officers of Butler's Rangers, with a number of children. Some of these people went down the lake to Montreal; but others remained at the post, and 'squatted' on the land. In 1780 Colonel Butler reports to Haldimand that four or five families have settled and built houses, and he requests that they be given seed early in the spring. In 1781 we know that a Loyalist named Robert Land had squatted on Burlington Bay, at the head of Lake Ontario. In 1783 Lieutenant Tinling was sent to Niagara to survey lots, and Sergeant Brass of the 84th was sent to build a saw-mill and a grist-mill. At the same time Butler's Rangers, who were stationed at the fort, were disbanded; and a number of them were induced to take up land. They took up land on the west side of the river, because, although, according to the terms of peace, Fort George was not given up by the British until 1796, the river was to constitute the boundary between the two countries. A return of the rise and progress of the settlement made in May 1784 shows a total of forty-six settlers (that is, heads of families), with forty-four houses and twenty barns. The return makes it clear that cultivation had been going on for some time. There were 713 acres cleared, 123 acres sown in wheat, and 342 acres waiting to be sown; and the farms were very well stocked, there being an average of about three horses and four or five cows to each settler.

With regard to the settlement at Detroit, there is not much evidence available. It was Haldimand's intention at first to establish a large settlement there, but the difficulties of communication doubtless proved to be insuperable. In the event, however, some of Butler's Rangers settled there. Captain Bird of the Rangers applied for and received a grant of land on which he made a settlement; and in the summer of 1784 we find Captain Caldwell and some others applying for deeds for the land and houses they occupied. In 1783 the commanding officer at Detroit reported the arrival from Red Creek of two men, 'one a Girty, the other McCarty,' who had come to see what encouragement there was to settle under the British government. They asserted that several hundred more would be glad to come if sufficient inducements were offered them, as they saw before them where they were nothing but persecution. In 1784 Jehu Hay, the British lieutenant-governor of Detroit, sent in lists of men living near Fort Pitt who were anxious to settle under the British government if they could get lands, most of them being men who had served in the Highland and 60th regiments. But it is safe to assume that no large number of these ever settled near Detroit, for when Hay arrived in Detroit in the summer of 1784, he found only one Loyalist at the post itself. There had been for more than a generation a settlement of French Canadians at Detroit; but it was not until after 1791 that the English element became at all considerable.

It has been estimated that in the country above Montreal in 1783 there were ten thousand Loyalists, and that by 1791 this number had increased to twenty-five thousand. These figures are certainly too large. Pitt's estimate of the population of Upper Canada in 1791 was only ten thousand. This is probably much nearer the mark. The overwhelming majority of these people were of very humble origin. Comparatively few of the half-pay officers settled above Montreal before 1791; and most of these were, as Haldimand said, 'mechanics, only removed from one situation to practise their trade in another.' Major Van Alstine, it appears, was a blacksmith before he came to Canada. That many of the Loyalists were illiterate is evident from the testimony of the Rev. William Smart, a Presbyterian clergyman who came to Upper Canada in 1811: 'There were but few of the U. E. Loyalists who possessed a complete education. He was personally acquainted with many, especially along the St Lawrence and Bay of Quinte, and by no means were all educated, or men of judgment; even the half-pay officers, many of them, had but a limited education.' The aristocrats of the 'Family Compact' party did not come to Canada with the Loyalists of 1783; they came, in most cases, after 1791, some of them from Britain, such as Bishop Strachan, and some of them from New Brunswick and Nova Scotia, such as the Jarvises and the Robinsons. This fact is one which serves to explain a great deal in Upper Canadian history.

CHAPTER XI

COMPENSATION AND HONOUR

Throughout the war the British government had constantly granted relief and compensation to Loyalists who had fled to England. In the autumn of 1782 the treasury was paying out to them, on account of losses or services, an annual amount of 40,280 pounds over and above occasional payments of a particular or extraordinary nature amounting to 17,000 pounds or 18,000 pounds annually. When peace had been concluded, and it became clear that the Americans had no intention of making restitution to the Loyalists, the British government determined to put the payments for their compensation on a more satisfactory basis.

For this purpose the Coalition Government of Fox and North appointed in July 1783 a royal commission 'to inquire into the losses and services of all such persons who have suffered in their rights, properties, and professions during the late unhappy dissensions in America, in consequence of their loyalty to His Majesty and attachment to the British Government.' A full account of the proceedings of the commission is to be found in the Historical View of the Commission for Inquiry into the Losses, Services, and Claims of the American Loyalists, published in London in 1815 by one of the commissioners, John Eardley Wilmot. The commission was originally appointed to sit for only two years; but the task which confronted it was so great that it was found necessary several times to renew the act under which it was appointed; and not until 1790 was the long inquiry brought to an end. It was intended at first that the claims of the men in the Loyalist regiments should be sent in through their officers; and Sir John Johnson, for instance, was asked to transmit the claims of the Loyalists settled in Canada. But it was found that this method did not provide sufficient guarantee against fraudulent and exorbitant claims; and eventually members of the commission were compelled to go in person to New York, Nova Scotia, and Canada.

The delay in concluding the work of the commission caused great indignation. A tract which appeared in London in 1788 entitled The Claim of the American Loyalists Reviewed and Maintained upon Incontrovertible Principles of Law and Justice drew a black picture of the results of the delay:

It is well known that this delay of justice has produced the most melancholy and shocking events. A number of sufferers have been driven into insanity and become their own destroyers, leaving behind them their helpless widows and orphans to subsist upon the cold charity of strangers. Others have been sent to cultivate the wilderness for their subsistence, without having the means, and compelled through want to throw themselves on the mercy of the American States, and the charity of former friends, to support the life which might have been made comfortable by the money long since due by the British Government; and many others with their families are barely subsisting upon a temporary allowance from Government, a mere pittance when compared with the sum due them.

Complaints were also made about the methods of the inquiry. The claimant was taken into a room alone with the commissioners, was asked to submit a written and sworn statement as to his losses and services, and was then cross-examined both with regard to his own losses and those of his fellow claimants. This cross-questioning was freely denounced as an 'inquisition.'

Grave inconvenience was doubtless caused in many cases by the delay of the commissioners in making their awards. But on the other hand it should be remembered that the commissioners had before them a portentous task. They had to examine between four thousand and five thousand claims. In most of these the amount of detail to be gone through was considerable, and the danger of fraud was great. There was the difficulty also of determining just what losses should be compensated. The rule which was followed was that claims should be allowed only for losses of property through loyalty, for loss of offices held before the war, and for loss of actual professional income. No account was taken of lands bought or improved during the war, of uncultivated lands, of property mortgaged to its full value or with defective titles, of damage done by British troops, or of forage taken by them. Losses due to the fall in the value of the provincial paper money were thrown out, as were also expenses incurred while in prison or while living in New York city. Even losses in trade and labour were discarded. It will be seen that to apply these rules to thousands of detailed claims, all of which had to be verified, was not the work of a few days, or even months.

It must be remembered, too, that during the years from 1783 to 1790 the British government was doing a great deal for the Loyalists in other ways. Many of the better class received offices under the crown. Sir John Johnson was appointed superintendent of the Loyalists in Canada, and then superintendent of Indian Affairs; Colonel Edmund Fanning was made lieutenant-governor of Nova Scotia; Ward Chipman became solicitor-general of New Brunswick. The officers of the Loyalist regiments were put on half-pay; and there is evidence that many were allowed thus to rank as half-pay officers who had no real claim to the title. 'Many,' said the Rev. William Smart of Brockville, 'were placed on the list of officers, not because they had seen service, but as the most certain way of compensating them for losses sustained in the Rebellion'; and Haldimand himself complained that 'there is no end to it if every man that comes in is to be considered and paid as an officer.' Then every Loyalist who wished to do so received a grant of land. The rule was that each field officer should receive 5,000 acres, each captain 3,000, each subaltern 2,000, and each non-commissioned officer and private 200 acres. This rule was not uniformly observed, and there was great irregularity in the size of the grants. Major Van Alstine, for instance, received only 1,200 acres. But in what was afterwards Upper Canada, 3,200,000 acres were granted out to Loyalists before 1787. And in addition to all this, the British government clothed and fed and housed the Loyalists until they were able to provide for themselves. There were those in Nova Scotia who were receiving rations as late as 1792. What all this must have cost the government during the years following 1783 it is difficult to compute. Including the cost of surveys, official salaries, the building of saw-mills and grist-mills, and such things, the figures must have run up to several millions of pounds.

When it is remembered that all this had been already done, it will be admitted to be a proof of the generosity of the British government that the total of the claims allowed by the royal commission amounted to 3,112,455 pounds.

The grants varied in size from 10 pounds, the compensation paid to a common soldier, to 44,500 pounds, the amount paid to Sir John Johnson. The total outlay on the part of Great Britain, both during and after the war, on account of the Loyalists, must have amounted to not less than 6,000,000 pounds, exclusive of the value of the lands assigned.

With the object possibly of assuaging the grievances of which the Loyalists complained in connection with the proceedings of the royal commission, Lord Dorchester (as Sir Guy Carleton was by that time styled) proposed in 1789 'to put a Marke of Honor upon the families who had adhered to the unity of the empire, and joined the Royal Standard in America before the Treaty of Separation in the year 1783.' It was therefore resolved that all Loyalists of that description were 'to be distinguished by the letters U. E. affixed to their names, alluding to their great principle, the unity of the empire.' The land boards were ordered to preserve a registry of all such persons, 'to the end that their posterity may be discriminated from future settlers,' and that their sons and daughters, on coming of age, might receive grants of two hundred acre lots. Unfortunately, the land boards carried out these instructions in a very half-hearted manner, and when Colonel John Graves Simcoe became lieutenant-governor of Upper Canada, he found the regulation a dead letter. He therefore revived it in a proclamation issued at York (now Toronto), on April 6, 1796, which directed the magistrates to ascertain under oath and to register the names of all those who by reason of their loyalty to the Empire were entitled to special distinction and grants of land. A list was compiled from the land board registers, from the provision lists and muster lists, and from the registrations made upon oath, which was known as the 'Old U. E. List'; and it is a fact often forgotten that no one, the names of some of whose ancestors are not inscribed in that list, has the right to describe himself as a United Empire Loyalist.

CHAPTER XII

THE AMERICAN MIGRATION

From the first the problem of governing the settlements above Montreal perplexed the authorities. It was very early proposed to erect them into a separate province, as New Brunswick had been erected into a separate province. But Lord Dorchester was opposed to any such arrangement. 'It appears to me,' he wrote to Lord Sydney, 'that the western settlements are as yet unprepared for any organization superior to that of a county.' In 1787, therefore, the country west of Montreal was divided into four districts, for a time named Lunenburg, Mecklenburg, Nassau, and Hesse. Lunenburg stretched from the western boundary of the province of Quebec to the Gananoqui; Mecklenburg, from the Gananoqui to the Trent, flowing into the

Bay of Quinte; Nassau, from the Trent to a line drawn due north from Long Point on Lake Erie; and Hesse, from this line to Detroit. We do not know who was responsible for inflicting these names on a new and unoffending country. Perhaps they were thought a compliment to the Hanoverian ruler of England. Fortunately they were soon dropped, and the names Eastern, Midland, Home, and Western were substituted.

This division of the settlements proved only temporary. It left the Loyalists under the arbitrary system of government set up in Quebec by the Quebec Act of 1774, under which they enjoyed no representative institutions whatever. It was not long before petitions began to pour in from them asking that they should be granted a representative assembly. Undoubtedly Lord Dorchester had underestimated the desire among them for representative institutions. In 1791, therefore, the country west of the Ottawa river, with the exception of a triangle of land at the junction of the Ottawa and the St Lawrence, was erected by the Constitutional Act into a separate province, with the name of Upper Canada; and this province was granted a representative assembly of fifteen members.

The lieutenant-governor appointed for the new province was Colonel John Graves Simcoe. During the war Colonel Simcoe had been the commanding officer of the Queen's Rangers, which had been largely composed of Loyalists, and he was therefore not unfitted to govern the new province. He was theoretically under the control of Lord Dorchester at Quebec; but his relations with Dorchester were somewhat strained, and he succeeded in making himself virtually independent in his western jurisdiction. Though he seemed phlegmatic, he possessed a vigorous and enterprising disposition, and he planned great things for Upper Canada. He explored the country in search of the best site for a capital; and it is interesting to know that he had such faith in the future of Upper Canada that he actually contemplated placing the capital in what was then the virgin wilderness about the river Thames. He inaugurated a policy of building roads and improving communications which showed great foresight; and he entered upon an immigration propaganda, by means of proclamations advertising free land grants, which brought a great increase of population to the province.

Simcoe believed that there were still in the United States after 1791 many people who had remained loyal at heart to Great Britain, and who were profoundly dissatisfied with their lot under the new American government. It was his object to attract these people to Upper Canada by means of his proclamations; and there is no doubt that he was partly successful. But he also attracted many who had no other motive in coming to Canada than their desire to obtain free land grants, and whose attachment to the British crown was of the most recent origin. These people were freely branded by the original settlers as 'Americans'; and there is no doubt that in many cases the name expressed their real sympathies.

The War of the Revolution had hardly been brought to a conclusion when some of the Americans showed a tendency to migrate into Canada. In 1783, when the American Colonel Willet was attempting an attack on the British garrison at Oswego, American traders, with an impudence which was superb, were arriving at Niagara. In 1784 some rebels who had attempted to pose as Loyalists were ejected from the settlements at Cataraqui. And after Simcoe began to advertise free land grants to all who would take the oath of allegiance to King George, hundreds of Americans flocked across the border. The Duc de la Rochefoucauld, a French emigre who travelled through Upper Canada in 1795, and who has given us the best account of the province at that time, asserted that there were in Upper Canada many who falsely profess an attachment to the British monarch and curse the Government of the Union for the mere purpose of getting possession of the lands.' 'We met in this excursion,' says La Rochefoucauld in another place, 'an American family who, with some oxen, cows, and sheep, were emigrating to Canada. "We come," said they, "to the governor," whom they did not know, "to see whether he will give us land." "Aye, aye," the governor replied, "you are tired of the federal government; you like not any longer to have so many kings; you wish again for your old father" (it is thus the governor calls the British monarch when he speaks with Americans); "you are perfectly right; come along, we love such good Royalists as you are; we will give you land."'

Other testimony is not lacking. Writing in 1799 Richard Cartwright said, 'It has so happened that a great portion of the population of that part of the province which extends from the head of the Bay of Kenty upwards is composed of persons who have evidently no claim to the appellation of Loyalists.' In some districts it was a cause of grievance that persons from the States entered the province, petitioned for lands, took the necessary oaths, and, having obtained possession of the land, resold it, pocketed the money, and returned to build up the American Union. As late as 1816 a letter appeared in the Kingston Gazette in which the complaint is made that 'people who have come into the country from the States, marry into a family, and obtain a lot of wild land, get John Ryder to move the landmarks, and instead of a wild lot, take by force a fine house and barn and orchard, and a well-cultivated farm, and turn the old Tory (as he is called) out of his house, and all his labor for thirty years.'

Never at any other time perhaps have conditions been so favourable in Canada for land-grabbing and land-speculation as they were then. Owing to the large amount of land granted to absentee owners, and to the policy of free land grants announced by Simcoe, land was sold at a very low price. In some cases two hundred acre lots were sold for a gallon of rum. In 1791 Sir William Pullency, an English speculator, bought 1,500,000 acres of land in Upper Canada at one shilling an acre, and sold 700,000 acres later for an average of eight shillings an acre. Under these circumstances it was not surprising that many Americans, with their shrewd business instincts, flocked into the country.

It is clear, then, that a large part of the immigration which took place under Simcoe was not Loyalist in its character. From this, it must not be understood that the new-comers were not good settlers. Even Richard Cartwright confessed that they had 'resources in themselves which other people are usually strangers to.' They compared very favourably with the Loyalists who came from England and the Maritime Provinces, who were described by Cartwright as 'idle and profligate.' The great majority of the American settlers became loyal subjects of the British crown; and it was only when the American army invaded Canada in 1812, and when William Lyon Mackenzie made a push for independence in 1837, that the non-Loyalist character of some of the early immigration became apparent.

CHAPTER XIII

THE LOYALIST IN HIS NEW HOME

The social history of the United Empire Loyalists was not greatly different from that of other pioneer settlers in the Canadian forest. Their homes were such as could have been seen until recently in many of the outlying parts of the country. In Nova Scotia and New Brunswick some of the better class of settlers were able to put up large and comfortable wooden houses, some of which are still standing. But even there most of them had to be content with primitive quarters. Edward Winslow was not a poor man, as poverty was reckoned in those days. Yet he lived in rather meagre style. He described his house at Granville, opposite Annapolis, as being 'almost as large as my log house, divided into two rooms, where we are snug as pokers.' Two years later, after he had made additions to it, he proposed advertising it for sale in the following terms: 'That elegant House now occupied by the Honourable E. W., one of His Majesty's Council for the Province of New Brunswick, consisting of four beautiful Rooms on the first Floor, highly finished. Also two spacious lodging chambers in the second story--a capacious dry cellar with arches &c. &c. &c.' In Upper Canada, owing to the difficulty of obtaining building materials, the houses of the half-pay officers were even less pretentious. A traveller passing through the country about Johnstown in 1792 described Sir John Johnson's house as 'a small country lodge, neat, but as the grounds are only beginning to be cleared, there was nothing of interest.'

The home of the average Loyalist was a log-cabin. Sometimes the cabin contained one room, sometimes two. Its dimensions were as a rule no more than fourteen feet by eighteen feet, and sometimes ten by fifteen. The roofs were constructed of bark or small hollowed basswood logs, overlapping one another like tiles. The windows were as often as not covered not with glass, but with oiled paper. The chimneys were built of sticks and clay, or rough unmortared stones, since bricks were not procurable; sometimes there was no chimney, and the smoke was allowed to find its way out through a hole in the bark roof. Where it was impossible to obtain lumber, the doors were made of pieces of timber split into rough boards; and in some cases the hinges and latches were made of wood. These old log cabins, with the chinks between the logs filled in with clay and moss, were still to be seen standing in many parts of the country as late as fifty years ago. Though primitive, they seem to have been not uncomfortable; and many of the old settlers clung to them long after they could have afforded to build better. This was doubtless partly due to the fact that log-houses were exempt from the taxation laid on frame, brick, and stone structures.

A few of the Loyalists succeeded in bringing with them to Canada some sticks of furniture or some family heirlooms. Here and there a family would possess an ancient spindle, a pair of curiously-wrought fire-dogs, or a quaint pair of hand-bellows. But these relics of a former life merely served to accentuate the rudeness of the greater part of the furniture of the settlers. Chairs, benches, tables, beds, chests, were fashioned by hand from the rough wood. The descendant of one family has described how the family dinner-table was a large stump, hewn flat on top, standing in the middle of the floor. The cooking was done at the open fireplace; it was not until well on in the nineteenth century that stoves came into common use in Canada.

The clothing of the settlers was of the most varied description. Here and there was one who had brought with him the tight knee-breeches and silver-buckled shoes of polite society. But many had arrived with only what was on their backs; and these soon found their garments, no matter how carefully darned and patched, succumb to the effects of time and labour. It was not long before the settlers learnt from the Indians the art of making clothing out of deer-skin. Trousers made of this material were found both comfortable and durable. 'A gentleman who recently died in Sophiasburg at an advanced age, remembered to have worn a pair for twelve years, being repaired occasionally, and at the end they were sold for two dollars and a half.' Petticoats for women were also made of deer-skin. 'My grandmother,' says one descendant, 'made all sorts of useful dresses with these skins, which were most comfortable for a country life, and for going through the bush [since they] could not be torn by the branches.' There were of course, some articles of clothing which could not readily be made of leather; and very early the settlers commenced growing flax and raising sheep for their wool. Home-made linen and clothing of linsey-woolsey were used in the settlements by high and low alike. It was not until the close of the eighteenth century that articles of apparel, other than those made at home of flax and wool, were easily obtainable. A calico dress was a great luxury. Few daughters expected to have one until it was bought for their wedding-dress. Great efforts were always made to array the bride in fitting costume; and sometimes a dress, worn by the mother in other days, amid other scenes, was brought forth, yellow and discoloured with the lapse of time.

There was little money in the settlements. What little there was came in pay to the soldiers or the half-pay officers. Among the greater part of the population, business was carried on by barter. In Upper Canada the lack of specie was partly overcome by the use of a kind of paper money. 'This money consists of small squares of card or paper, on which are printed promissory notes for various sums. These notes are made payable once a year, generally about the latter end of September at Montreal. The name of the merchant or firm is subscribed.' This was merely an extension of the system of credit still in use with country merchants, but it provided the settlers with a very convenient substitute for cash. The merchants did not suffer, as frequently this paper money was lost, and never presented; and cases were known of its use by Indians as wadding for their flint-locks.

Social instincts among the settlers were strongly marked. Whenever a family was erecting a house or barn, the neighbours as a rule lent a helping hand. While the men were raising barn-timbers and roof-trees, the women gathered about the quilting-frames or the spinning-wheels. After the work was done, it was usual to have a festival. The young men wrestled and showed their prowess at trials of strength; the rest looked on and applauded. In the evening there was a dance, at which the local musician scraped out tuneless tunes on an ancient fiddle; and there was of course hearty eating and, it is to be feared, heavy drinking.

Schools and churches were few and far between. A number of Loyalist clergy settled both in Nova Scotia and in Upper Canada, and these held services and taught school in the chief centres of population. The Rev. John Stuart was, for instance, appointed chaplain in 1784 at Cataraqui; and in 1786 he opened an academy there, for which he received government aid. In time other schools sprang up, taught by retired soldiers or farmers who were incapacitated for other work. The tuition given in these schools was of the most elementary sort. La Rochefoucauld, writing of Cataraqui in 1795, says: 'In this district are some schools, but they are few in number. The children are instructed in reading and writing, and pay each a dollar a month. One of the masters, superior to the rest in point of knowledge, taught Latin; but he has left the school, without being succeeded by another instructor of the same learning.' 'At seven years of age,' writes the son of a Loyalist family, 'I was one of those who patronized Mrs Cranahan, who opened a Sylvan Seminary for the young idea in Adolphustown; from thence, I went to Jonathan Clark's, and then tried Thomas Morden, lastly William Faulkiner, a relative of the Hagermans. You may suppose that these graduations to Parnassus was [sic] carried into effect, because a large amount of knowledge could be obtained. Not so; for Dilworth's Spelling Book, and the New Testament, were the only books possessed by these academies.'

The lack of a clergy was even more marked. When Bishop Mountain visited Upper Canada in 1794, he found only one Lutheran chapel and two Presbyterian churches between Montreal and Kingston. At Kingston he found 'a small but decent church,' and about the Bay of Quinte there were three or four log huts which were used by the Church of England missionary in the neighbourhood. At Niagara there was a clergyman, but no church; the services were held in the Freemasons' Hall. This lack of a regularly-ordained clergy was partly remedied by a number of itinerant Methodist preachers or 'exhorters.' These men were described by Bishop Mountain as 'a set of ignorant enthusiasts, whose preaching is calculated only to perplex the understanding, to corrupt the morals, to relax the nerves of industry, and dissolve the bands of society.' But they gained a very strong hold on the Loyalist population; and for a long time they were familiar figures upon the country roads.

For many years communications both in New Brunswick and in Upper Canada were mainly by water. The roads between the settlements were little more than forest paths. When Colonel Simcoe went to Upper Canada he planned to build a road running across the province from Montreal to the river Thames, to be called Dundas Street. He was recalled, however, before the road was completed; and the project was allowed to fall through. In 1793 an act was passed by the legislature of Upper Canada 'to regulate the laying out, amending, and keeping in repair, the public highways and roads.' This threw on the individual settler the obligation of keeping the road across his lot in good repair; but the large amount of crown lands and clergy reserves and land held by speculators throughout the province made this act of little avail. It was not until 1798 that a road was run from the Bay of Quinte to the head of Lake Ontario, by an American surveyor named Asa Danforth. But even this government road was at times impassable; and there is evidence that some travellers preferred to follow the shore of the lake.

It will be seen from these notes on social history that the Loyalists had no primrose path. But after the first grumblings and discontents, poured into the ears of Governor Haldimand and Governor Parr, they seem to have settled down contentedly to their lot; and their life appears to have been on the whole happy. Especially in the winter, when they had some leisure, they seem to have known how to enjoy themselves.

In the winter season, nothing is more ardently wished for, by young persons of both sexes, in Upper Canada, than the setting in of frost, accompanied by a fall of snow. Then it is, that pleasure commences her reign. The sleighs are drawn out. Visits are paid, and returned, in all directions. Neither cold, distance, or badness of roads prove any impediment. The sleighs glide over all obstacles. It would excite surprise in a stranger to view the open before the Governor's House on a levee morning, filled with these carriages. A sleigh would not probably make any great figure in Bond street, whose silken sons and daughters would probably mistake it for a turnip cart, but in the Canadas, it is the means of pleasure, and glowing healthful exercise. An overturn is nothing. It contributes subject matter for conversation at the next house that is visited, when a pleasant raillery often arises on the derangement of dress, which the ladies have sustained, and the more than usual display of graces, which the tumble has occasioned.

This picture, drawn in 1793 by a nameless traveller, is an evidence of the courage and buoyancy of heart with which the United Empire Loyalists faced the toils and privations of life in their new home.

Not drooping like poor fugitives they came In exodus to our Canadian wilds, But full of heart and hope, with heads erect And fearless eyes victorious in defeat.

BIBLIOGRAPHICAL NOTE

It is astonishing how little documentary evidence the Loyalists left behind them with regard to their migration. Among those who fled to England there were a few who kept diaries and journals, or wrote memoirs, which have found their way into print; and some contemporary records have been published with regard to the settlements of Nova Scotia and New Brunswick. But of the Loyalists who settled in Upper and Lower Canada there is hardly one who left behind him a written account of his experiences. The reason for this is that many of them were illiterate, and those who were literate were so occupied with carving a home for themselves out of the wilderness that they had neither time nor inclination for literary labours. Were it not for the state papers preserved in England, and for a collection of papers made by Sir Frederick Haldimand, the Swiss soldier of fortune who was governor of Quebec at the time of the migration, and who had a passion for filing documents away, our knowledge of the settlements in the Canadas would be of the most sketchy character.

It would serve no good purpose to attempt here an exhaustive account of the printed sources relating to the United Empire Loyalists. All that can be done is to indicate some of the more important. The only general history of the Loyalists is Egerton Ryerson, The Loyalists of America and Their Times (2 vols., 1880); it is diffuse and antiquated, and is written in a spirit of undiscriminating admiration of the Loyalists, but it contains much good material. Lorenzo Sabine, Biographical Sketches of Loyalists of the American Revolution (2 vols., 1864), is an old book, but it is a storehouse of information about individual Loyalists, and it contains a suggestive introductory essay. Some admirable work on the Loyalists has been done by recent American historians. Claude H. Van Tyne, The Loyalists in the American Revolution (1902), is a readable and scholarly study, based on extensive researches into documentary and newspaper sources. The Loyalist point of view will be found admirably set forth in M. C. Tyler, The Literary History of the American Revolution (2 vols., 1897), and The Party of the Loyalists in the American Revolution (American Historical Review, I, 24). Of special studies in a limited field the most valuable and important is A. C. Flick, Loyalism in New York (1901); it is the result of exhaustive researches, and contains an excellent bibliography of printed and manuscript sources. Other studies in a limited field are James H. Stark, The Loyalists of Massachusetts and the Other Side of the American Revolution (1910), and G. A. Gilbert, The Connecticut Loyalists (American Historical Review, IV, 273).

For the settlements of Nova Scotia and New Brunswick, the most important source is The Winslow Papers (edited by W. O. Raymond, 1901), an admirably annotated collection of private letters written by and to Colonel Edward Winslow. Some of the official correspondence relating to the migration is calendared in the Historical Manuscript Commission's Report on American Manuscripts in the Royal Institution of Great Britain (1909), Much material will be found in the provincial histories of Nova Scotia and New Brunswick, such as Beamish Murdoch, A History of Nova Scotia or Acadie (3 vols., 1867), and James Hannay, History of New Brunswick (2 vols., 1909), and also in the local and county histories. The story of the Loyalists of Prince Edward Island is contained in W. H. Siebert and Florence E. Gilliam, The Loyalists in Prince Edward Island (Proceedings and Transactions of the Royal Society of Canada, 3rd series, IV, ii, 109). An account of the Shelburne colony will be found in T. Watson Smith, The Loyalists at Shelburne (Collections of the Nova Scotia Historical Society, VI, 53).

For the settlements in Upper and Lower Canada, the most important source is the Haldimand Papers, which are fully calendared in the Reports of the Canadian Archives from 1884 to 1889. J. McIlwraith, Sir Frederick Haldimand (1904), contains a chapter on 'The Loyalists' which is based upon these papers. The most important secondary source is William Canniff, History of the Settlement of Upper Canada (1869), a book the value of which is seriously diminished by lack of reference to authorities, and by a slipshod style, but which contains a vast amount of material preserved nowhere else. Among local histories reference may be made to C. M. Day, Pioneers of the Eastern Townships (1863), James Croil, Dundas (1861), and J. F. Pringle, Lunenburgh or the Old Eastern District (1891). An interesting essay in local history is L. H. Tasker, The United Empire Loyalist Settlement at Long Point, Lake Erie (Ontario Historical Society, Papers and Records, II). For the later immigration reference should be made to D. C. Scott, John Graves Simcoe (1905), and Ernest Cruikshank, Immigration from the United States into Upper Canada, 1784-1812 (Proceedings of the Thirty-ninth Convention of the Ontario Educational Association, 263).

An authoritative account of the proceedings of the commissioners appointed to inquire into the losses of the Loyalists is to be found in J. E. Wilmot, Historical View of the Commission for Inquiry into the Losses, Services, and Claims of the American Loyalists (1815).

For the social history of the Loyalist settlements a useful book is A 'Canuck' (M. G. Scherk), Pen Pictures of Early Pioneer Life in Upper Canada (1905). Many interesting notes on social history will be found also in accounts of travels such as the Duc de la Rochefoucauld-Liancourt, Travels through the United States of North America, the Country of the Iroquois, and Upper Canada (1799), The Diary of Mrs John Graves Simcoe (edited by J. Ross Robertson, 1911), and Canadian Letters: Description of a Tour thro' the Provinces of Lower and Upper Canada in the Course of the Years 1792 and '93 (The Canadian Antiquarian and Numismatic Journal, IX, 3 and 4).

An excellent index to unprinted materials relating to the Loyalists is Wilfred Campbell, Report on Manuscript Lists Relating to the United Empire Loyalists, with Reference to Other Sources (1909).

See also in this Series: The Father of British Canada; The War Chief of the Six Nations.

END